THE ENTREPRENEUR'S
WEEKLY NIETZSCHE

THE ENTREPRENEUR'S WEEKLY NIETZSCHE

A Book for Disruptors

DAVE JILK and BRAD FELD

LIONCREST
PUBLISHING

THE ENTREPRENEUR'S WEEKLY NIETZSCHE
A Book for Disruptors

ISBN		
	978-1-5445-2141-1	*Hardcover*
	978-1-5445-2140-4	*Paperback*
	978-1-5445-2139-8	*Ebook*
	978-1-5445-2094-0	*Audiobook*

Cartoon illustrations by Neil Kohney

To our fathers, Stanley Feld and Dave Jilk, who gave each of us our first introduction to entrepreneurship, and who were willing to send us to MIT, where we began our friendship and collaborations.

TABLE OF CONTENTS

FOREWORD

Nietzsche is a troubling and troublesome philosopher. In different decades and contexts, even scholars have formed radically different interpretations of his work. Nietzsche lends himself to these conflicting interpretations because he philosophizes with an aphoristic hammer and an intense literary style. While the many subjects of his attacks are clear, the reasons and implications of his critique can lead to many different interpretations. Nietzsche deploys this approach in pursuit of bold originality and self-creation. This is what makes him such a good patron philosopher for entrepreneurs.

Entrepreneurs frequently seek to disrupt an industry by creating new products and services based on changing technologies and markets. Nietzsche sought to disrupt the philosophy of his day through stylistic aphorisms that challenged staid, traditional academic methods. Entrepreneurs develop their companies with new company cultures and new business models. Nietzsche developed his philosophy through a shift of frame, a metamorphosed question, a poetical imperative. Entrepreneurs compete by speed, originality, and strategy—providing modern solutions to classic problems. Nietzsche competed by tearing down old systems of philosophy—replacing old idols (values, religions) with modern humanity.

As Dave and Brad note in this book, Nietzsche himself dismissed commercial activity and those who engaged in it as crass and dully unambitious. Most of the businesspeople in his day, after all, were local shopkeepers and bourgeoisie, locked into the rote patterns and conventions of daily commerce. Whereas Nietzsche, in contrast, felt that the highest pursuit of the human soul was to seek human evolution: evolution of identity, of culture, of new mind. Even more specifically, evolution to absolute originality: the creation of the never-seen-before.

In these aspirations, Nietzsche encapsulates entrepreneurship. Build the new. Renovate institutions. View markets and customers as evolutionary—and join them in their evolution. Nietzsche was a disruptor, in the ways that entrepreneurs are also disruptors. Where philosophers and philologists studied the classics to honor and entrench history, Nietzsche wanted to cast down those idols to create a new philosophy. Where companies and industrialists have achieved a market position, they work to keep that industry and market roughly where it is. In contrast, entrepreneurs strive to revolutionize industries through new products and services based upon new technologies and alternative business models.

But beyond anointing an outstanding philosopher of entrepreneurship, why is this book important?

Nietzsche also looked forward—to what humanity could and should become: *Ecce Homo* ("Behold the Man"). In parallel, some of the best entrepreneurs are also great humanists. Since we often experience entrepreneurs first and foremost as capitalists or technologists, some may find this surprising. But thinking about who we are as humans and who we can become parallels how entrepreneurs shape the evolution of products, customers, and markets.

This is partially why philosophy can be fundamental to entrepreneurship. There are, of course, many entrepreneurs and businesspeople who think that philosophy is useless or worse. In this view, entrepreneurs and philosophers reside on opposite ends of a utility spectrum: entrepreneurs are pragmatic doers with common-sense theories designed to fulfill the actual wants and needs of the public they serve; philosophers generate grand but abstract theories that may be intellectually impressive but do not survive engagement with the world.

Surely there are philosophers who do lose the trees for the forest. But when you put thought and action together, you have a very powerful combination.

One of my favorite expressions is: in theory, there is no difference between theory and practice. The implication: in practice, there are significant differences between theory and practice. Nevertheless, both are critically important. Theory-driven practice—where you improve your theory from practice—is the strongest approach. Philosophy teaches you how to think in general theories. Philosophy teaches you precision in thought and language. Philosophy teaches you how to construct a theory, test it for truth, and then evolve that theory. And so does entrepreneurship if you're doing it right!

Other disciplines—from physics to economics to psychology—focus on more specific domains and teach you how to evolve theories in those domains. But philosophy's generality is the attribute that makes it a preferred part of an entrepreneur's toolset. Entrepreneurs frequently are doing something original with their business: a new way of acquiring customers or engaging customers, a new technological platform, a new business strategy or operational approach, a new business model. These innovations generally escape current theories and frameworks, so they need new formulations to express them— as goals, as strategies, as new systems. Philosophy provides the general terms to formulate a new theory.

Finally, philosophy mostly concerns itself with human nature. Philosophy is the love of wisdom, the pursuit of truth and knowledge. Theories of human nature underlie this pursuit: Who are we such that we seek truth and knowledge? What sorts of truth can we grasp? How do we act with respect to those truths?

I believe that a theory of human nature underlies every entrepreneurial pursuit. Who are we, such that we will want this new product or service over existing products and services? Who are we, such that this new means of acquiring customers will succeed? Who are we, such that we will remain deeply engaged with this new product or service?

Because I believe that entrepreneurial projects require a specific theory about human nature, I frequently start with a philosophical observation when I deliver public talks on investing. For example, for nearly two decades I have been saying that investing in the consumer internet means investing in one or more of the seven deadly sins. Business school students usually think that you become adept at investing by learning about concepts like Customer Acquisition Cost (CAC), Lifetime Value (LTV), operating margins, competitive differentiation, and so on. However, every entrepreneurial project targets a future CAC or LTV, so how do you get there? Who are we, such that we will stay engaged with this product at scale? Philosophy helps you think sharply about your theory of human nature and how it ties to your entrepreneurial goals.

Returning to Nietzsche, let's examine why he in particular is such an apt patron philosopher for entrepreneurs. Nietzsche was rebelling against a stultifying philosophical practice that exalted the past—specifically the ideals and images of former thinkers and former leaders. He wanted to refocus on the now, on what humanity was and what it could become.

As part of his rebellion, Nietzsche philosophized with a hammer: he wanted to destroy the old mindsets that locked people into the past, and thus better equip them to embrace the possibility of the new. Nietzsche's desire to shift mindsets is also why he emphasized new styles of argument. Whereas most philosophers would typically open an argument in a classical form or by reviewing a historical great, Nietzsche would lead with an arresting aphorism or a completely new mythological narrative.

He was, above all else, a disruptor of pieties and convention, always in search of new and original ways to be contrarian and right, never satisfied with the status quo.

This is exactly the kind of mindset entrepreneurs should adopt. This is why a daily practice of philosophy can be the way that an entrepreneur moves from good to great. And, why a daily practice of Nietzsche is a great practice of philosophy for entrepreneurs.

In *Twilight of the Idols*, Nietzsche exclaims, "To live alone, you must be an animal or a god—says Aristotle. He left out the third case: you must be both—a philosopher."

The entrepreneur's version might go like this: "Aristotle says that to envision a new product that changes the model, one must either be a mad person or genius. Forgetting the third case, both—an entrepreneur."

In the end, Nietzsche's fierce allegiance to the new made him troublesome—and valuable. Change always brings trouble—for example, the trouble that entrepreneurs make when they create "disruption." To achieve a new and better future, you must first reject the old. One of America's most effective modern civil rights heroes, the late Congressman John Lewis, had a great way to describe trouble as essential. "Get into good trouble, necessary trouble," he used to say. Good trouble is how we progress, in markets and in societies.

Reid Hoffman
Entrepreneur, Investor, Occasional Philosopher
March 2021

INTRODUCTION

Nietzsche? For entrepreneurs?

It was the end of January 1988, about nine months since we had embarked on turning Brad's solo consulting shop, Feld Technologies, into a real business. We were fraternity brothers and close friends and opened our first office directly across the street from our fraternity chapter house in Cambridge. We planned to use smart yet inexpensive software developers to build business application software. We employed half a dozen programmers, most of whom were undergraduates from our fraternity working part-time. We didn't have any financing except for Brad's credit card and the $10 with which we had purchased our common stock.

Dave walked into Brad's office after calculating preliminary financial results for January. Up to this point, we had mostly broken even, but the news was grim: we had lost $10,000 in one month. We had not seen it coming, and it took some effort for us to untangle what had gone wrong. Dave had been spending most of his time managing the part-time developers, who were primarily working on future products, instead of billing hours to clients. Brad had been selling computer equipment, which had low gross profit margins, instead of billing hours to clients. Much of our revenue for the month had come from one highly productive though erratic undergraduate developer, Mike, who was working on a billable client project.

Before we had a chance to figure out what to do, Mike quit, citing a need to focus on his studies. Now we had no choice: we fired everyone, shut down our month-to-month office, sold all the office furnishings, and moved the business to our apartments in downtown Boston. It was gut-wrenching. Brad wondered whether we had failed just as we got started. Dave worried about paying rent. We had long discussions about the future of the business, including whether or not to continue.

But we did have billable projects. We no longer had to spend our time managing people and had figured out where our bread was buttered. Results were good enough in February to calm our nerves and even better in March. Just as important, we had learned some crucial lessons and settled on a very different idea about how we would move forward with the business. The experience of hitting bottom and the lessons we learned became deeply ingrained in our brains and our company culture as we more methodically and progressively built the firm.

Fast-forward thirty years, when we were in the midst of writing this book, and Dave was reading *Thus Spoke Zarathustra*. He encountered a passage that said the highest mountains rise from the sea, and that fact is "inscribed...on the walls of their summits." Because of our experience at Feld Technologies—and many times since—we knew immediately that this had to be a chapter in the book. We imagined the solace and instruction it might have offered us to have seen (and understood) this quote, to have read a short essay like the one in our chapter *Hitting Bottom*, where the starkness and promise of the situation are presented in black and white, or to have heard Walter Knapp's story of the crash and rebirth of Sovrn, a genuinely disruptive company.

That is how we wrote most of the chapters and how this project began. In reading Nietzsche, we noticed ideas that reminded us of situations, questions, and concerns that frequently arose in our entrepreneurial and venture investment experience. Nietzsche had a way with words, and we found that some ideas were nicely encapsulated and phrased. We started playing with expanding upon his pithy aphorisms and gathering stories from entrepreneurs, and it clicked.

Feld Technologies never became a disruptive company, despite our ambitions. It plateaued at around $2 million in revenue before we sold it in 1993. Because we had built a solid foundation for a certain kind of success, we never again hit a deep low point, and consequently never again had the painful opportunity to rethink our premises. This point, too, is covered in *Hitting Bottom* and illustrates why we did not just skip Nietzsche, write some essays, and assemble some entrepreneur stories. Nietzsche—sitting or walking alone, in pain, almost blind—thought deeply and managed to share these thoughts with the world. We tried to follow his lead, thinking hard and pondering additional angles and situations to which the quote might apply. We want you to do the same, as you keep in mind that Nietzsche's works have been highly influential throughout the 20th century and into the 21st.

In business and entrepreneurship literature, inspiration is sometimes more helpful than instruction. Though there is plenty of how-to information in this book, we aim to give you food for thought from a different perspective. We address issues of leadership, motivation, morals, creativity, culture, strategy, conflict, and knowledge. We push you to think about what you and your enterprise are made of. We expect you to question and ponder these ideas, not just put them into action. If we are successful, you will sometimes get angry and at other times feel pride. At times you will wonder what you really know, and at other times you will charge forward. We hope that the combination of Nietzsche's colorful language, our elaborations, and some stories from entrepreneurs will offer you intellectual, emotional, and entrepreneurial inspiration.

Nietzsche was not a fan of commercial activity or businesspeople. He saw the former as crass and the latter as lacking nobility. However, we suspect that if Nietzsche were alive today, he would view entrepreneurs differently. He adored intensity and fervor, deeply valued those who create things, and wrote at length about "free spirits" who do not feel bound to tradition or cultural norms. Nietzsche viewed his mission as the "revaluation of all values," and he intended to disrupt the entire moral tradition of Europe in the late 19th century.

Our subtitle, *A Book for Disruptors*, echoes the subtitles of *Human, All-Too-Human: A Book for Free Spirits* and *Thus Spoke Zarathustra: A Book for All and None*. We chose it because our intended audience consists of entrepreneurs who aspire to completely change or create a new industry, rather than those who are merely starting a business. Nietzsche's character Zarathustra says, "Preserve me from all small victories!...Spare me for one great victory!" This is the mindset of the disruptive entrepreneur. If you are disrupting by creating and creating by disrupting, Friedrich Nietzsche would have been a fan of yours, and so are we.

Nietzsche is difficult to read, and many of his popular quotes are impenetrable. We attempt to make Nietzsche accessible through short quotes that we adapt to 21st-century English. Only a small fraction of the words in this book are Nietzsche's, so don't worry; it won't kill you—it will make you stronger.

Nietzsche is frequently misunderstood, and some mainstream impressions of him or his philosophy are discomfiting. You may have heard that his ideas played a role in the Third Reich. You may have seen recent articles that he is an inspiration for the "alt-right." We have observed that most strong claims about Nietzsche's substantive philosophy are suspect, especially when they come from non-scholars. With a little effort, one can find actual language from Nietzsche's works showing that the most common worries and assertions are contrived or overblown. To support this and address concerns you might have, we've included an appendix titled *Don't Believe Everything You Hear about Nietzsche*. There we examine the journalistic history of the alleged alt-right connection and discover that it is mostly clickbait. To be clear, we would not have written this book if we thought these attributions had merit.

In Silicon Valley and other startup communities, the philosophy of Stoicism is popular and trendy. At some point in this project, we realized that Nietzsche's approach represents a productive and healthy sequel to Stoicism, particularly for the disruptive entrepreneur. For Nietzsche, the Stoic willingness to bear burdens, stay focused on the task, and do what is required regardless of discomfort is only the first stage of personal development. That stage is necessary, but not sufficient, to enable one to reimagine the world and create entirely new values and value propositions. If you follow Stoic principles, this book will offer a glimpse into how you might build on that foundation. If you are not familiar with Stoicism, don't worry, as it overlaps considerably with Nietzsche's first stage, and there are plenty of similar ideas to be found here.

Several successful entrepreneurs studied philosophy in college, including Reid Hoffman of LinkedIn, Peter Thiel of PayPal, and Stewart Butterfield of Flickr and Slack. Many others find guidance, solace, or mental stimulation in reading philosophy or using philosophical approaches to thinking about the world. Though we hope we offer you insight into Nietzsche and his philosophy, our contribution is not a substitute for reading his actual work. Digging deeper into Nietzsche can be transformative and enjoyable. If you do, you will experience considerably more discomfort—and deep thoughts—than our curated sample and simple interpretations can offer.

HOW THE BOOK IS ORGANIZED

The book contains fifty-two individual chapters (one for each week) and is divided into five major sections (*Strategy, Culture, Free Spirits, Leadership,* and *Tactics*). Each chapter begins with a quote from one of Nietzsche's works, using a public domain translation, followed by our own adaptation of the quote to 21st-century English. Next is a brief essay applying the quote to entrepreneurship. About two-thirds of the chapters include a narrative by or about an entrepreneur we know (or know of), telling a concrete story from their personal experience as it applies to the quote, the essay, or both.

The word "weekly" is in the title to emphasize the importance of giving each quote and the ensuing essay and example time to percolate and synthesize with your own business situation. Rather than grinding through chapter after chapter, we encourage you to reflect on the quote, essay, and narrative during the course of a workweek. Does it fit something that is happening within your company? Does it seem helpful, or does it seem contrary to what you need to do? Are there other people within your organization who would benefit from reading, thinking about, or discussing the chapter? Don't just skim the chapter—chew on it awhile.

If you have not read Nietzsche and do not regularly read hundred-year-old English, we encourage you to start each chapter by reading our adaptation of the quote. Only then read the actual quote. Return to both of them after you read the essay. Put energy into associating the aphorisms with these ideas to help you remember the idea as you go about your business. Don't be bashful about reading the chapter a second or third time throughout the week.

You do not need to read the chapters in any particular order, and they have no prerequisites or dependencies. Where there are interrelationships among them, we indicate these in the text. Flip to a chapter that piques your interest and start with that.

The first two major sections, *Strategy* and *Culture*, are about your business. The next two, *Free Spirits* and *Leadership*, are about you as a leader and entrepreneur. *Tactics* is mostly about communication. Chapters within each major section are ordered to have a lightweight, logical flow.

Neither the major sections nor the book as a whole constitutes a comprehensive treatment of either Nietzsche or entrepreneurship. Nietzsche was not writing about entrepreneurship, yet the breadth of his work that can be applied to entrepreneurship is striking. Nonetheless, there are major gaps. Even with respect to his own ostensible topics, Nietzsche's works are not systematically comprehensive.

We've included three appendices, none of which are required to understand the book. Appendix 1 contains a biography and an overview of those who influenced and were influenced by Nietzsche. Appendix 2 is the essay *Don't Believe Everything You Hear about Nietzsche*. These offer introductory insight into his work and life. Appendix 3 cites the sources and translators of the Nietzsche quotes we have selected.

OUR INTERPRETIVE APPROACH

We are not Nietzsche scholars nor is this a scholarly treatment of Nietzsche. We also are not entrepreneurship academics, and this is not a scholarly treatment of entrepreneurship questions. However, we do have considerable experience in entrepreneurship, both as founders and investors. Our goal is to bring together some ideas from Nietzsche, our own experience and reasoning, and some examples from entrepreneurs we know, to provide you with perspective and inspiration around your entrepreneurial journey.

We chose Nietzsche quotes that reflect important aspects of entrepreneurship, giving preference to those that are pithy and colorful while avoiding opaque ones. While we looked for potential insights broadly throughout Nietzsche's works, we expect that we missed some great quotes.

We rely on surface interpretations of Nietzsche's words and metaphors rather than the intricate allusions and subtle symbolism discussed in literary criticism circles. Such deeper interpretations tend to be disputed and are outside our scope of writing a book that helps you think about yourself and your business. We have written the essays in a prescriptive fashion, but that does not mean you should necessarily agree with us.

We have taken liberties in applying Nietzsche's ideas to the domain of entrepreneurship. Many of the quotes refer to people in the arts: artists, poets, and composers. Nietzsche's notion of a leader is usually a philosophical leader (such as he viewed himself) or a political leader. We see entrepreneurs as another kind of creator, leader, and disruptor and believe Nietzsche's ideas are sufficiently deep and general to accommodate our novel application of them. In a few cases, the Nietzsche quote inspired the essay, but we did not directly apply or interpret it.

You will also find that some of the entrepreneur narratives are not an exact fit with either Nietzsche's words or our elaboration. We did not provide the narratives to "drive the point home," though some accomplish that. Instead, they illustrate where a particular entrepreneur's mind traveled after reading the quote and essay. Neither should you feel limited in the concerns and ideas the chapter might address or inspire for you.

The narratives are real stories, not artificial parables. Nietzsche frequently suggested that our abstractions and general principles are a form of illusion and often misleading. Thus, these narratives do not merely add color—they provide a concrete and independent angle on the subject matter. As Gilles Deleuze said in his classic book *Nietzsche and Philosophy*, "The anecdote is to life what the aphorism is to thought: something to interpret." On that same note, the word "narrative" implies interpretation, and we chose it for that reason. We have not attempted to fact-check these stories, and they should not be construed as an attempt at objective journalism. Rather, each one is an entrepreneur's interpretation of something important that happened.

We have no illusions that this book is something Nietzsche would have liked: he said, "The worst readers are those who act like plundering soldiers. They take out some things that they might use, cover the rest with filth and confusion, and blaspheme about the whole." Hopefully, we have not done much of the latter, but we were surely opportunistic in selecting just what we could use.

Finally, keep in mind what Nietzsche said about his own work: "Granted that this also is only interpretation—and you will be eager enough to make this objection?—well, so much the better." Even his claim that everything is interpretation is just another interpretation.

STRATEGY

We begin with "strategy", an overused and misused word in entrepreneurship. A simple Google search leads down a rabbit hole of classical definitions, Sun Tzu's *The Art of War*, missives by Peter Drucker, and an entire book by Michael Porter (*Competitive Strategy*) that more MBAs seem to reference than any other book, ever.

While Nietzsche wasn't a management theorist or a leader, his instincts about strategy were prescient. This is because his insights were based on lasting elements of human nature and psychology, as well as a keen knowledge of history. He instinctively understood the difference between an incremental change and a fundamental innovation. He recognized that there is no single right way to do things. Most importantly, he knew that change takes time, even when it seems to appear overnight.

The word "planning" is often left out of strategy, unless one refers to the "strategic planning process." Nietzsche offers us perspective on both the importance and difficulty of planning, especially in the context of ambitious progress and disruption. When trying to accomplish something, one must understand the difference between milestones and goals.

Remember, Nietzsche's writing can be challenging. Read it slowly and out loud to yourself. Consider writing it on paper to reinforce what he is saying and to help you recall the chapter later. Then repeat it after you've read the chapter.

DOMINATION

> "How we must Conquer.—We ought not to desire victory if we only have the prospect of overcoming our opponent by a hair's breadth. A good victory makes the vanquished rejoice, and must have about it something divine which spares humiliation."

In other words: We should not aim for narrow victories. A good victory is so awe-inspiring and overwhelming that even the loser is impressed and does not feel humiliated by the loss.

Large, established companies with mature products tend to focus on incremental improvements and advantages. A tenth-of-a-point increase in market share or a two-cent increase in gross profit on a low-margin product can mean millions of dollars in net income.

Optimizations like these are not the province of entrepreneurs. Your opportunities are not in incremental, nor even substantial, improvement. You need to completely disrupt the status quo and offer a new way of doing things that is at least ten times better than the norm. That is not an exaggeration—"10x" is a conceptual rule of thumb for some investors, not only for their investment return, but also in the amount of improvement the product must offer.

There are many practical reasons for this. Established businesses have tried-and-true operational processes, organizational structures, industry relationships, and selling tactics. You have none of these. There are considerable risks in setting them up, and a single error can overwhelm the advantage your product provides.

An incumbent has a brand. Even if that brand is not fully respected, customers see it as the "devil they know." All change comes with tradeoffs, and customers will resist making a change for a relatively small potential gain. Investors look for companies that can quickly become large, which can only happen if what you offer is dramatically better. Employees are much more motivated by "changing the world" than by minor tweaks; it is one of the reasons they join startups.

These disruptive improvements are not always the result of new technology. Sometimes new organizational processes, service delivery modes, or sales and marketing approaches can offer large improvements. New approaches to existing problems in these areas can be as dramatic and overwhelming as entirely new products.

It is unlikely that the incumbent competitors will "*rejoice*" when you disrupt their business and push their mature product line into decline. But, when executives and individual contributors from those incumbents want to join your company, you will know that you have created something "*divine*." Since they are familiar with the business domain, some of them will realize that it is the future. They are not humiliated that your company is beating them—instead, they find new inspiration in the industry that has been their home.

When you think about an opportunity, try to imagine one that is so compelling that the forward-looking employees of the incumbents will get excited about your offering. You might even try asking a few of them.

For more on finding opportunities that create disruptive change, see *Doing the Obvious*, *Maturity as Play*, and *Deviance*. For another angle on thinking big, see *Serial Entrepreneurship*.

FINDING YOUR WAY

> " 'This—is now MY way,—where is yours?'
> Thus did I answer those who asked me 'the
> way.' For THE way—it does not exist! "

*In other words: People often ask me how to do something. I
tell them how I do it, but then I ask them how they're going
to do it. Because there is no one way to do something.*

Nietzsche's philosophy emphasizes that there are many ways to look at things and different ways to live. His approach is called "perspectivism," and we apply it to entrepreneurship by suggesting that there are many ways to build a business and to be an entrepreneur. In this book, we intentionally offer conflicting advice, and we mention the idea of "mentor whiplash" as observed in the Techstars program. In the end, regardless of the advice you receive, you have to make the final decision on the path you and your company take.

Have you ever wondered how experienced businesspeople know what the right answer is in a given situation? They often seem quite certain about the correct path, and they may recommend that you take that same path. They have business experience that guides their beliefs, but have they done controlled, unbiased studies with a representative sample? Have they fully examined the range of conditions under which their view is valid? Almost certainly not. In a few cases, there may be academic research showing that certain approaches work better or worse. Even then, it can be difficult to nail down the precise actions one should take or the range of circumstances in which they are applicable.

Much of the time, businesspeople base their experience and wisdom on anecdotes and ungrounded core beliefs rather than hard empirical evidence. The field of machine learning shows that inference is more effective with more data, so when someone has seen many examples, an intuitive view potentially has some validity, and statistics come into play.

For example, if an executive has built large, successful sales teams at multiple organizations, her instincts on hiring salespeople probably have some merit. In contrast, someone who has built one large, successful business might be able to help you think about your own strategy, and might believe that they know the right strategy for you, but can't possibly know with certainty that it is correct. Investors who have seen many strategies may have better insights into the specifics of potential strategies. However, never forget that experience is about the past, the world is always changing, and the rate of change is accelerating.

The practice of entrepreneurship is more professional and standardized than a few decades ago. Growth of standardized financing sources, including not only venture capital but also angel networks and accelerators, makes it seem like there is one right way to do things. They all use similar term sheets and comparable board structures. They tend to focus on comparable technology categories. This partially arises from the desire of investors to make their own lives easier, as well as to improve the chances of business success as they define success. The quintessential contrarian entrepreneur of today is one who bootstraps and builds a business without outside financing or accelerator programs.

Even if there is one right way to run your business (and probably there is not), no one actually knows for sure what it is. Agendas and idiosyncratic experiences will color any advice you receive. Thus you must find your own way.

There is a fine line between doing things your own way and making rookie mistakes. First-time entrepreneurs often insist that the way the world works in some respect is wrong and endeavor to do it differently in their own business. Frequently the result is not that the world is changed or improved, but rather that the entrepreneur learns the hard way why the world is how it is. Sometimes the best advice from experienced people consists of simply telling you how everyone does something. This in itself has great value.

Any area in which you attempt to innovate will require considerable effort. If your business not only offers a new product, but also uses an entirely new organizational structure, a novel distribution approach, and a unique financing strategy, good luck to you. Chances are high that while you fight the inevitable resistance in one area, you lose the battle in others. If you want to conquer Europe, don't try to do it on two fronts at once.

There is a tradeoff. There is no single right way to build and run your business. You must find your own way. But this does not mean that you can do it "any old way" and expect it to work. If you innovate in too many areas at once, you will be crushed by the obstacles you find in every direction. Nietzsche might appreciate this sort of adversity; but remember, he was little known and sold few books during his active writing career.

For more on the implications of going your own way, see *Deviance*, *Two Types of Leaders*, and *Consequences*. For more on how experienced advisors can help you to avoid rookie mistakes, see *Maturity*. For more on assessing the advice your receive from investors and others, see *Strong Beliefs* and *Red Hot*.

A Narrative from Daniel Benhammou

FOUNDER AND CEO, ACYCLICA

My first startup was a business called Hamilton Signal. I took a small amount of family & friends money as startup financing, but mostly I bootstrapped it. The absence of capital seemed to inhibit our growth, and definitely took a personal toll as I constantly had to make ends meet. When I sold Hamilton it was still a small company, though I did get to keep most of the proceeds.

When I started Acyclica several years ago, I approached investors (both angels and venture capitalists) with my plan, hoping that investment capital would enable me to move faster and avoid daily cash flow pressure. They were reluctant to believe that a business selling technology to public agencies to improve traffic and reduce congestion would be a solid business. They were concerned about both the long sales cycle when working with public agencies, and uncertain about our ability to deploy and scale fast enough. As usual, they also fretted about market size and differentiation.

I was determined at the time that it was possible, and that by building and selling a product, I could show investors the potential in this market. So I bootstrapped again; we grew Acyclica to $3 million in revenue, with *an established customer base and distribution network. I was ready to go back to the VCs. I worked on my pitch deck, consulted friends and advisers, and started meeting with prospective investors.*

The experience was remarkably similar to my earlier attempts. Potential investors were nervous about investing in a company with public sector clients, despite our demonstrated success. After six months focused on raising money, I realized I could not afford to keep pursuing dead ends. I returned to building my business directly. With limited capital, we focused on working through partners. This has allowed us to scale sales, distribution and support in a manner that is cost-effective and efficient, but is not capital intensive.

Still, all those meetings with VCs, private equity investors, and potential acquirers challenged me with good questions that I might not have otherwise asked myself. The thinking process led us to focus on the strategic value of the data we were collecting. Though we continue to work primarily with public sector end-users, the business itself has transformed into a data business. I remain optimistic that the true value of Acyclica will be built on the data and our strong network of public-sector clients.

DOING THE OBVIOUS

"Also Worthy of a Hero.—Here is a hero who did
nothing but shake the tree as soon as the fruits
were ripe. Do you think that too small a thing?
Well, just look at the tree that he shook."

*In other words: Some people are heroes because
they did something that now seems obvious. Does
that make it less heroic? Just look at the result.*

A startup succeeds by being in the right place at the right time. How it
got there, and how difficult it was, does not count for much from the
perspective of the business.

In today's competitive world, the process of starting new ventures
and seeking opportunities is professionalized and methodical. It is
unusual to simply find a *"tree as soon as the fruits were ripe,"* in other
words, an unsolved business problem ready to be solved. Often, other
entrepreneurs have seen the same opportunity. If not, investors may

see the absence of competitors as a red flag. It could indicate that there is no market, it is too early, or the entrepreneur has little awareness of what others are doing.

Some entrepreneurs do manage to find undiscovered ripe fruit. Often they are engaged in the industry or in a role where they are domain experts. This vantage point enables them to see new opportunities as they arise. It gives them insight into the solutions that will work and be attractive to potential customers who face those problems. Even though many others in the domain may notice the problem, few are equipped or motivated to find those solutions.

If you are a domain expert, you do not need to look further or do anything harder than solve a big problem that you see every day. If you are an entrepreneur but are not a domain expert, you would do well to find one as a partner. This partner will enable you to find opportunities that are ready to be exploited and will save you considerable pain by avoiding mistakes that stem from a lack of familiarity with the domain. Ultimately, a partner who is a domain expert can save you months or years of learning the industry structure, its assumptions, and its important players. Most importantly, it helps you address a problem that is ready to be solved.

An entrepreneur without domain expertise can nevertheless find a ready opportunity before others do. This involves luck combined with rapid experimentation, hypothesis testing, and iteration. Lean and agile startups begin by targeting a general area and exploring variations in a product and the market to find product/market fit. Sometimes there is an opportunity nearby, but sometimes there is not. Sometimes the entrepreneur is the first to find it, but other times she is not.

Finding the *"ripe fruit"* is only the beginning. Next, you have to *"shake the tree."* You have to commit to the idea and build the product, customer base, and organization. Not everyone is willing to do that, and it is what makes you an entrepreneur...and a hero.

For more on the process of finding ripe opportunities, see *Information, Hitting Bottom,* and *Maturity as Play.*

A Narrative from Jason Mendelson

FOUNDING PARTNER EMERITUS, FOUNDRY GROUP
AND CO-FOUNDER, SRS ACQUIOM

After you read this story you'll see why I don't consider myself a hero. I suppose anyone who has the gumption to actually start something instead of just complaining about it deserves some credit, but I was just solving a very big problem for myself.

When a company is acquired, it is extremely rare for all of the purchase price to be paid out at the closing. There is almost always an "escrow" of some of the funds to protect the buyer in case some of the representations in the deal were invalid. A simple example might be that the selling company owed a vendor substantially more money than the balance sheet reflected. There might also be an earn-out or other post-closing processes that need to take place. To manage this, the transaction documents appoint a "shareholder representative" to represent the interests of the selling share-holders. Historically, this appointment was something of an afterthought, decided at the last minute by "volunteering" one of the selling shareholders.

In 2000 I was hired as General Counsel of Mobius Venture Capital (at the time called Softbank Technology Ventures). Mobius was a large fund, with $2.5 billion under management. At that time, there were a few small venture firms that had a general counsel, but no large ones. When our investments were acquired, it was a natural outcome that I was appointed shareholder representative. It was just part of the job of being the law-yer. Within a few years I was shareholder representative for around thirty companies. I was probably one of the first people to experience this situation en masse because previously the assignments would have been spread around more. It got to be a significant amount of work, but manageable, and I became a domain expert in shareholder representation.

I was the shareholder representative in one large, fateful deal with a $200 million escrow. The transaction had specified a date by which the buyer had to make claims against the escrow. A few days after the deadline I received a claim for 100% of the escrow. I told the buyer that they were out of luck, they had made the claim too late. So they sued the selling company and they sued me personally for $150 million. This was a new twist on the role.

At the time, I was in the process of moving to Colorado, both to continue my role with Mobius as well as to co-found a new fund, Foundry Group, with some of my partners. One of my errands was to get a new phone with a Colorado number, so I visited the AT&T store. They declined my credit: despite having an otherwise great credit report, the lawsuit was on my record. This was my moment of epiphany – I could not get a new phone because I was a shareholder representative!

Though I had committed to the Foundry Group, our fundraising was not going particularly well at that point. I decided to start a business that would solve my shareholder representative problem – and who knows? – could it also serve as a backup plan in case we were not able to raise our first fund? I knew that other general counsels were starting to have the same shareholder rep problem, but more importantly, the shareholders of the seller were usually at a disadvantage against the buyer because they rarely had an experienced representative. A "go-to" third party shareholder representative would be advantageous in almost all acquisition transactions. This was the "ripe fruit" that SRS Acquiom would pick from the tree (SRS stands for "Shareholder Representative Services.")

I was committed to Foundry, so I could not run SRS myself, and needed to find a co-founder and CEO. I had a number of criteria and realized that *my friend and colleague Paul Koenig was the perfect fit. The only problem was that Paul was only a year or two into running his own law firm – with his name on the door. It took him about three weeks to come around.*

SRS is now the dominant player in shareholder representative services. Paul is a great CEO, and he is a hero for having the courage to leave a stable and lucrative career as a law firm founder. Foundry raised its first fund in 2007 and I was able to hand off all my shareholder representative duties to SRS. I have never since been appointed to that role, and now I can get whatever phone or number I want.

OVERCOMING OBSTACLES

"Surprise at Resistance.—Because we have reached the point of being able to see through a thing we believe that henceforth it can offer us no further resistance—and then we are surprised to find that we can see through it and yet cannot penetrate through it. This is the same kind of foolishness and surprise as that of the fly on a pane of glass."

In other words: We think that if we understand something, we can surely overcome it. It surprises us when events play out as we expect, yet we cannot seem to do anything to change them. This is the same foolishness as a fly repeatedly hitting a window.

Sometimes entrepreneurship feels like an obstacle course. For every step you try to take forward, something blocks your path. You have to work through or around it, so your plans always take longer than expected.

Many entrepreneurs are optimists. You can see where you want to go, and you have confidence and enthusiasm to take you there. When an unanticipated obstacle arises, it surprises you. Nietzsche captures this sentiment well—one can almost hear the fly batting against the glass, trying to get out of the house. It can see its way forward, yet keeps getting surprised by the glass.

It is difficult to break this pattern. For your business to succeed, you need to set audacious goals for your team and achieve them. Yet you know that unforeseen obstacles will appear, some of which you cannot overcome just by trying harder. This sets up a conflict that is ripe to produce disappointment.

There is no silver bullet that solves this problem. The first step, though, is to stop being surprised and upset when it happens.

The second step is to learn to recognize when an obstacle cannot be overcome by persistence. Sometimes things just take longer than you expected. Other times you are taking the wrong approach. We can extend the pane of glass metaphor to illustrate. The window might be open, and it may just be a matter of finding that open corner. Or the window may be closed, and the only solution is to fly around the house looking for another exit. How long do you continue to dive into the same window before you look for another route?

There is no simple answer to this question either. However, by being aware that neither persistence nor a change of strategy always holds the right solution, you improve your chances. Sometimes experienced advisors can help you to assess what to do.

Don't be surprised when you fly into a window. And, when you do, think hard about when and to what extent you should change direction to get past it.

For more on experienced advisors, see *Maturity*. For different angles on persistence, see *Persistence*, *Patience in Disruption*, and *Resolute Decisions*.

A Narrative from Ralph Clark

CEO, SHOTSPOTTER

ShotSpotter builds a combination hardware and software system that detects, locates, and alerts on gunshots, both to reduce crime and save lives. When I joined the company as CEO, their sales and deployment strategy was a straightforward enterprise sale to municipalities. Customers were among the more technologically sophisticated cities and police departments in the United States. Once the sale was made and the devices and software installed, the customers were on their own, aside from technical support and maintenance.

This had seemed to the founding team like the obvious path to success, but sales were not ramping up. We had slammed into a window. To figure out why, I spent considerable time with our existing customers as well as prospective customers who had not adopted the technology. What I learned was fascinating. The customers represented themselves as technologically adept, but when I looked closer, these skills tended to be narrowly focused and have limited resources. Their practical ability to work with a new and different technology was low.

I also learned that they were not really using the system actively. When I probed, and listened empathetically to the message between the lines, it seemed like they were uncomfortable with the position that the system put them in. Not every alert was a real gunshot, and someone had to be responsible for making that assessment. If they responded to a false positive, they wasted resources, and if they didn't respond to a true positive, lives could be lost. Because police departments are often unfairly held accountable for judgments made in a crisis, they resisted this new source of imperfect information.

My solution was to completely change the business model. I decided to offer ShotSpotter as a subscription managed service, in which we would manage all the software and deploy and maintain the hardware. Most importantly, we would have a central operations center that monitored all of the alerts triggered by the system, make an assessment in each case, and only report very high probability gunshot sounds to the applicable police department.

After coming up with this new strategy, which I believed would open the window, I slammed into an obstacle of my own. Our team was not fully on board with this pivot. They were not convinced I was reading the market correctly, and were prepared to keep trying the enterprise sales strategy, perhaps with some minor changes or just to try harder. Some resisted actively, others passively.

I made a further decision, which was even more difficult, that my new strategy was correct and that anyone who was not on board would not be moving forward with the company. I gave an all-hands talk where I explained that we had landed on a new shore and we were burning the ships. There would be no returning to the old strategy and we were betting the company on the new one. We lost a few people, but the culture of those remaining turned toward making the new strategy a success. Fortunately, it turned out to be correct, and ShotSpotter is now saving lives around the world.

PATIENCE IN DISRUPTION

" Small Doses.—If we wish a change to be as deep
and radical as possible, we must apply the remedy
in minute doses, but unremittingly for long periods.
What great action can be performed all at once? "

*In other words: To create radical change, we must
pursue it incrementally and consistently over a long
period of time. Rome wasn't built in a day.*

Your budding entrepreneurial organization is fast on its feet, and
you can change direction on a dime. Through firing and hiring, your
culture can be changed quickly and dramatically. You are in a hurry,
not just because you have the ambition to change the world, but
because you will run out of money if you don't achieve positive cash
flow or raise more financing. You have had some early success, and

through luck or force of will you have obtained early customers or good press.

You may be frustrated with how slow-moving and resistant to change the world is. A true disruption takes time. Amara's Law says, "we tend to overestimate the effect of a technology in the short run and underestimate the effect in the long run." Occasionally a fad will cause a product to succeed rapidly, but these successes often fade just as abruptly when the trend-followers move on to the next new thing. You can make a lot of money from a fad, but you have to get lucky in creating it and have exquisite timing in selling it. Disruption requires patience. Your strategy must take into account both the expected resistance and the time it will take for your solution to embed itself deeply into business processes or consumer lifestyles. Reliable paradigms like the Gartner Hype Cycle suggest that real change takes a long time, even in industries whose moment seems to have arrived.

In order to disrupt an industry, you have a big vision for your company and your products. You imagine business customers using your offerings across their organization or consumers using them multiple times a day in several aspects of their lives. While keeping your vision in mind, offer products that can be used easily and solve a single problem immediately. Customers must be able to obtain this benefit without adopting your entire vision. Press to get as many customers as you can this way, adding other narrow features as necessary to target different segments. Continue to add capabilities, focusing on those providing immediate benefit while aiming toward your vision. These *"minute doses"* will add up over time. Eventually, customers will change their behavior enough that you can start to sell the big vision to them.

Plan on this taking a decade. Bring on investors who understand your long view and have the wherewithal to support that effort. Plan

to keep your burn rate low while you are still in the early stages of the
"unremitting remedy."

For more on perseverance, see *Persistence, Sustaining Intensity,*
and *Obsession.* For more on executing on your vision, see *Genius* and
Planning.

A Narrative from Jenny Lawton
COO, TECHSTARS

I've been involved in disrupting an industry several times. In each case,
hurrying and optimizing for an early big outcome hurt the business.

My first technology company was Net Daemons Associates (NDA), a
professional services firm founded during the recession of the early 1990s.
As a company that supported computer networks, we capitalized on the
early Internet by working with Internet Service Providers. We were also a
pioneer in bringing web sites to life, with customers like Monster Board
(now Monster.com). NDA followed a growth trajectory similar to the early
growth of the Internet, but because we were bootstrapped, we had to live
by what we made. Though we grew rapidly and took advantage of the
Internet bubble, we never got out over our skis in terms of delivering a
technology or service that didn't have an already known demand.

In 1999, we realized that we were positioned in a valuable market cate-
gory and decided to make an exit. We entered into an acquisition by SAGE
Networks – a "rollup" with an overall mission to be the biggest web host-
ing and application service provider in the world. We were the 15th of 27
acquisitions.

The day after our acquisition closed, SAGE agreed to buy Interliant, the
largest Lotus Notes hosting company. This doubled the company's overall
size; we changed our name to Interliant and went public shortly after that.
We were flying high and riding the crest of a very large wave of disruption,

all under the safety of a stock market bubble. We continued rolling up web hosting companies as fast as we could find them.

At Interliant, the basics of business were relegated to a rainy day task. There would be plenty of time to make money and to understand the market dynamics. In those early days of the Internet, such routine issues felt like old hat. We were winning, and getting market share quickly was what mattered.

Like many others, we mistook our timelines for those of the rest of the world, so we missed. There were no tools to support Internet ubiquity. There were no real marketplaces. There was no easy way to do commerce online. Not everyone had a computer. Cell phones were still just phones. Moore's Law had not yet worked its magic on displays and batteries and processing power. We had indeed created the biggest web hosting company in the world, but we were so far ahead of the consumer adoption curve that it would be another ten years before the value of our market disruption could be realized.

The market bubble burst, and when the dust cleared we were in a new world. A world where the bottom line mattered again, and mere top line growth couldn't carry the day. Although we'd clearly disrupted a fast-growing market, we couldn't make the jump from flying high to operational success.

HITTING BOTTOM

" Whence come the highest mountains? So did
I once ask. Then did I learn that they come out
of the sea. That testimony is inscribed on their
stones, and on the walls of their summits. Out of
the deepest must the highest come to its height. "

*In other words: I wondered where the highest mountains
come from. I learned that they come out of the sea.
The evidence is in their rocks and on their summit
walls. The highest things must start very low.*

Achieving great success often requires that you first experience great pain. This is one of Nietzsche's core principles and is quite common in entrepreneurship. Many successful entrepreneurs have failed at least once. Many great companies have gone through a period during which their viability was in question. Is there a reason for this, or is it just statistics?

Most of us are not particularly reflective when things are going reasonably well. We think about our actions and make course corrections but are unlikely to question our basic premises. Why fix what ain't broke?

We dig deep when things are going badly or when we are feeling pain. This may mean looking at the fundamental assumptions of the business or looking at our own psychology and facing up to some dark truths about our own behavior.

If you find yourself at a low point, you have the opportunity to completely restructure your thinking. You can start by considering new values, new assumptions about the nature of the opportunity you are pursuing, and new views on your role as a leader. You might even reconsider whether you should be a leader or entrepreneur. Your previous approach was not working; perhaps an entirely new one will.

A deep reassessment does not guarantee success. It only gives you a chance. One rarely hears about all the companies and entrepreneurs who reached a low point, changed direction, and failed anyway. Most of the sea bottom stays beneath the surface. Still, this is a mechanism by which some of the greatest successes arise. The entrepreneurs undertook to genuinely question fundamental issues, this time with considerable experience. That experience is what Nietzsche means by "*that testimony is inscribed on their stones, and on the walls of their summits.*"

If you are at a low point, this notion serves as both consolation and guidance. But what if you are not at a low point— if, instead, you are experiencing modest success, what seems like a local maximum? This is one of the most difficult decisions in business. Risking the good to achieve the great requires a certain kind of disposition; it is also one of the most common disconnects between investors (who are looking for outsized returns) and entrepreneurs.

We know what Nietzsche would say, but then again, few people read his books while he was alive.

For more on learning and rebounding from failures, see *Serial Entrepreneurship, Information*, and *Wisdom from Experience*. For more on aiming high, see *Domination*. For more on consolation at a low point, see *Reflecting Your Light*.

A Narrative from Walter Knapp
CEO, SOVRN HOLDINGS

In 2010, I was COO of a company called Lijit. We figured out how to consolidate and auction-off vast amounts of unsold advertising inventory from our customers, thereby making them more money. With a solid and rapidly growing revenue base, we were able to sell the company to a larger and more established firm, Federated Media, with the possibility of an IPO on the horizon. Those were euphoric days.

Fast forward two years and the situation had changed considerably. The integration of our acquisition had not gone well, the Federated Media part of the business had suffered a major downturn, and several top executives were no longer with the firm. Eventually, I was offered the opportunity to take the reins as CEO.

We were able to sell the Federated Media business, clean up the balance sheet, and refocus the remaining team. It amounted to a total reset. The sale of our parent company left us with two important assets: a slug of cash in the bank, and a solid customer base – though we were still losing money. We re-started and changed the name of the company to Sovrn. The remaining employees had been through the growth, acquisition, the hopes of a massive upside and then the severe downturn rollercoaster. We were all "shell shocked," but we now had a fresh start, and I had high hopes for our future.

I couldn't have known, but that wasn't the low point. In early 2014 an "investigatory" article was published that claimed we were enabling fraudulent inventory to be purchased by advertisers. This was, and still is, a widespread problem in the industry, and we did have sophisticated systems in place to combat it. Still, given the sheer volumes in our network and the deviousness of the fraudsters, it's possible that some had slipped past our filters.

Despite the fact that the allegations were never proven, I took the situation to heart. I didn't want to be in the business of enabling illegal activity. We implemented draconian measures to cut any and all questionable traffic, even if it was potentially legitimate. Much of what we eliminated simply went to our competitors, who seemed to be less concerned about the potential fraud issue, and far more interested in the revenue they could gain.

Within three months our revenue run rate dropped by nearly 60%, and we were hemorrhaging cash. Employees, already on edge, were losing faith. We had no choice but to downsize and try to operate profitably at a smaller size. If I thought morale was low before, now with a layoff and precipitous drop in revenue, the team took on a touch of PTSD. One-time hopes for an IPO, turned into a day-to-day struggle simply to survive.

Then a funny thing happened. Our revenue began to grow, slowly at first, and then rapidly. Around the time we downsized, the advertising market had finally started to face up to the problem of traffic quality and the insidious presence of fraud. Both these factors greatly affected the value they received for their dollar. The buying algorithms big advertisers use saw that we were filtering more aggressively than our competitors. We became a more attractive path to reaching real people who were spending their time and attention on the content. Our customers, aiming for quality, were once again making more money through our services. We took a leap when we could least afford it and re-established trust. We gained business back, solidly based on an offering we could all be proud of. Momentum had returned.

We continued to grow rapidly. The business faces new headwinds today as every business does, but our insistence on quality and durability is now "inscribed on our stones." We risked everything by taking the high road, and it worked. The downturn was exceedingly painful, but it forced a brutal reassessment that laid a foundation for our present and future success.

SILENT KILLERS

"The greatest events—are not our noisiest, but our stillest hours. Not around the inventors of new noise, but around the inventors of new values does the world revolve; it revolves inaudibly."

In other words: The greatest events occur around quiet rather than noise. The world revolves silently around those who create new values, not those who produce an uproar.

———————

Do you spend a significant portion of your energy pursuing visibility and buzz for your business? Have you considered whether this is a worthwhile use of your time?

There is a school of thought that believes aggressive promotion is essential to success and growth, particularly in the technology industry. "Viral" services need to have the pump primed in order to get customers. Being seen as "hot" helps you raise capital at more attractive valuations. Being talked about makes it easier to attract employees and partners.

An alternative approach is to be a "silent killer." These are companies that mostly keep their heads down, work on their product, and serve their customers. They might be known in the geography where they are located or within their pertinent technology community. But they are not a household name, at least not yet. Whatever visibility they have gained came about through what they did, not what they said.

This is not a dispute about whether visibility can be helpful in the right times, places, and quantities. Rather, it is a question of what takes priority. Giving priority to creating buzz—*"inventing new noise"*—is a risky strategy. In doing this, you are borrowing enthusiasm against the future value that you intend to deliver. There is no escaping the fact that you eventually need to deliver value to customers and thereby enable investors, employees, and partners to share in that value.

If your company directs its energy and focus toward creating buzz, it is distracted from building products and understanding what makes customers successful. Worse, the excitement and adulation are addictive. You will find it tempting to keep doubling down. Meanwhile, it may take longer than you expect to find product/market fit. It may be difficult to create the product that is required to solve customer problems. If these or other delays occur, and you have built a high level of excitement and anticipation, the disappointment that will inevitably occur may be difficult to recover from.

Talk to customers, not the press. Energize your engineers, not journalists. Wait for the visibility to be pull, not push. When the journalists and bloggers reach out to you, and not the other way around, you can be sure you are an *"inventor of new values,"* and that is your *"great event."*

For more on resisting industry buzz, see *Seeing the Future*. For another aspect of the *"stillest hour,"* see *Introverts*. For more on not rushing your company's progress, see *Patience in Disruption*.

A Narrative from Mat Ellis
FOUNDER, CLOUDABILITY

Not all noise is promotional.

"I think we should lawyer up on this." The email sat in my inbox like the last cookie on a plate that nobody wants to take.

We'd recently turned our investment focus toward getting to market, after two years of intense emphasis on engineering and product. With a new head of sales came the inevitable wave of exits, as with any new executive.

At some point we became aware that a competitor was hiring or trying to hire every single ex-employee of ours. Non-compete agreements are unenforceable in our state; still, we had treated these folks very generously. The news was more of an emotional hit than anything more worrying, especially as it was generally the individuals who had been asked to leave who said yes. Those who had left voluntarily uniformly told the competitor where to go.

And this same competitor was trying to sign up for trial accounts. Our license agreement forbids reverse engineering and we don't want people poking around to see what we're up to. This went beyond just moving to a competitor – now you're using your knowledge of our systems to bypass filters intended to stop this. The pitchforks were out. Our team had had enough.

"The disloyalty was upsetting. But this is treachery! F*ck these guys." The emails were still there. And I had to decide what to do.

We invented our market category, and were the undisputed leaders until we failed to scale. A year or two of rebuilding mid-flight allowed new entrants to catch up, and now we found ourselves in a two- or three-way fight to the death.

We'd always taken the high road, as the ones who made this space. Ignore all the smoke. Our product will shine through. Seeing colleagues at a competitor was a new development. Our culture was strong; we hadn't ever really experienced this kind of disloyalty. Things had become personal.

"We need to discuss this at the next e-team." Another one.

I've always prided myself on being an emotionally aware leader. Sometimes you've got to do something because, well, leadership. The team needs you to do something, anything. I was pissed too. I had the email address for the latest turncoat, ready for me to send them a profound and stinging "I'm disappointed in you" note. That would likely never get written, because why would I? Nothing good would come of it. But boy, it would feel good!

Reflecting on what to do, I became aware that I had a deep conviction that we must continue to focus on our business, our customers, and not get distracted by this. There was no way we could get engaged in a legal and semi-public slanging match. It would achieve nothing and risk a bunch.

"Can you review this letter our lawyers have written to send to these traitors?"

This thing was getting a life of its own. Time to shut it down.

SEEING THE FUTURE

"Weather Prophets.—Just as the clouds reveal to us
the direction of the wind high above our heads, so
the lightest and freest spirits give signs of future
weather by their course. The wind in the valley
and the market-place opinions of today have no
significance for the future, but only for the past."

*In other words: The direction of the wind at high altitude is shown
by the motion of the clouds. Similarly, trends of the future are
shown by people who are light and free spirits. Current events
and common opinions tell us only about the past, not the future.*

———————

Your attention is a precious and limited resource. You must be careful about consuming unnecessary noise, and here Nietzsche uses the metaphor of the wind to make that point. He suggests that true visionaries are not immersed in day-to-day public squabbles and instead are operating on a different plane.

Many entrepreneurs feel drawn to the buzz of current events, especially in their business domain. A news item or a piece of punditry in your industry seems to have high relevance: it is about topics you understand and people or companies you know. The same goes for conversations at industry gatherings. These inputs could affect decisions you are about to make. Sometimes they also include a bit of drama, conflict, gossip, or even schadenfreude, which makes them even more intriguing and tempting, though not more useful.

People and companies have long capitalized on these psychological tendencies to vie for your attention. In the era of yellow journalism in the 1890s, newspapers artificially enhanced the relevance and drama with snappy and often negative or exaggerated headlines. More recently, with the rise of the Web, then blogs, then social media, and finally the revenue challenges of commercial media, competition for your attention has reached new heights. The *"wind in the valley"* is ferocious! Yet most of the information that comes to you this way is about the past. Even year-end predictions and rumors about what companies are planning rarely look far into the future.

You should be careful not to over-react to the latest news and gossip. Your business is not day-trading. In order to build a sustainable company over the long haul, you need a direction and a strategy that is largely independent of short-term fluctuations in attitudes and market conditions. This does not mean you should completely ignore current events. Rather, they should not have an undue influence on your company's behavior.

To understand where the clouds are going, spend a lot of time listening to your customers and prospective customers. Don't just ask them about what they need right now. Ask them where they think things are headed. They will not always be right or consistent, but if you synthesize what you hear, you might be able to get some traction on it. This might make you the *"freest spirit"* setting a course. Also, look toward others who are focused on the long term, who are not engaged directly in the public conversation, but show the direction by their actions. These are people who are the industry rather than those talking about the industry. Instead of stating their opinion on the future, they are actively moving in that direction.

For a discussion of managing noise of your own making, see *Silent Killers*. For another angle on keeping up with the market, see *Two Kinds of Leaders*. For more on taking the long view, see *Patience in Disruption* and *Milestones*. For more on domain expertise in a market, see *Doing the Obvious*.

A Narrative from Laura Rich
CO-FOUNDER AND CEO, STREET FIGHT

Street Fight was (and is, under new ownership) a niche digital media company focusing on issues around hyper-local marketing. It's no secret that media in general have been struggling and searching for new business models. Companies in transitional markets often watch each other to see what is working, and we were not an exception.

When we conceived of Street Fight in 2011, digital media companies were still pretty focused on advertising revenue. But advertising was anemic across the board, and new business models were emerging. One of these models added events and research products into the mix, and one company in particular, in a market adjacent to ours, was seeing a lot of success with it. We launched Street Fight with that model in mind.

The ad revenue was fine. The events were amazing. But the research was hard. There was an appetite for the research topics we produced, but the revenue model was tricky. In the early days, client-sponsored reports drove most of our research work and revenue. This was profitable but did not seem scalable, sustainable, or strategic.

About eighteen months in, we looked to raise a financing round to fund expansion, and the "wind in the valley" started to blow. Research was a big part of the discussion: some potential investors were gung-ho on a subscription model for research, drawn to the ideal of a stable revenue base. Others urged us to abandon research altogether, insisting there was too much free information available for anything paid to be of actual value. In the midst of this, the company on which we had modeled ourselves imploded spectacularly, brought down by a faulty revenue model for its research.

Our revenue model was different in important details, and we picked up their former research director in the fallout, so we had further insight into avoiding their missteps. We passed on funding, but continued to put resources against research, and it continued to struggle. The market noise continued when a new competitor entered our space and claimed to be killing it with a subscription model that looked very similar to that which doomed the other company. It brought new – and possibly false – hope for research, not just to us but to a whole collection of companies focused on niche audiences.

We never did get the research revenue model quite right. In the end we learned that success was less about the business model, and more about knowing what the customers want and delivering that. All the noise around business model "best practices" was a distraction for us; a close and dynamic relationship with customers was what really drove our success.

INFORMATION

"The thinker sees in his own actions attempts and questionings to obtain information about something or other; success and failure are answers to him first and foremost. To vex himself, however, because something does not succeed, or to feel remorse at all—he leaves that to those who act because they are commanded to do so, and expect to get a beating when their gracious master is not satisfied with the result."

In other words: A thinker sees his actions as a way of obtaining information. For him, success and failure are just answers to questions he has asked. Because of this attitude, failure does not bother him, and he has no regrets about it. Regrets are for followers and subordinates who will be reprimanded or punished by their dissatisfied bosses.

In a stable business, gaining knowledge almost always takes a back seat to immediate results. Such firms already have the answers they need—at least for the moment. Entrepreneurship is different. Innovation and disruption require exploration of the unknown. Intentionally acquiring knowledge, often through experiments, of which many will fail, is an inherent part of the process. This knowledge is ultimately the means to success. In Silicon Valley and other startup communities, there is an acceptance, understanding, and even promotion of failure as a vehicle for learning and self-development.

Despite this, you are not likely to hear unsophisticated investors tell you that it's fine if the business fails, as long as you learn something. They feel you should have gotten all that failure and learning out of the way before they invested! In contrast, sophisticated investors will be more tranquil about failure and will often be supportive of you on your next journey, assuming they believe you've learned something from your failure.

The ramifications of failure can also be personal. You may have worked two years without a salary. During this time, your spouse supported the family, you mortgaged your home and spent all the cash you took out, and you took investments from family and friends. No matter what you learn, it will be small consolation if the business fails and you *"get a beating."*

Nietzsche's quote refers to *"the thinker,"* so you might wonder whether his complete dismissal of the need for success applies to you, as someone who is in the arena. But this tension between discovery and results operates in every field where new ground is being covered. Scientists must publish experiments that show interesting and important new results or they do not get tenure or funding. Artists, poets, and musicians must find an audience or their passion turns into a hobby. Even philosophers want their ideas to have influence, illustrating that the *"gracious master"* can be oneself.

Entrepreneurs can be their own harshest critics. When they fail, they may feel their ego crushed and drive for achievement diminished. But in all of these endeavors, to make disruptive progress, one must take risks and periodically fail.

Approaches like the lean startup model take a positive step toward reconciling the tension. In this model, you perform small experiments and have many small failures as you pivot repeatedly toward product/ market fit. As long as you, your investors, and your co-founders or employees are not too attached to a particular strategy, this can work well for finding the best opportunity. Nevertheless, the approach only goes so far. Eventually, you need to find a direction that works, or you will run out of money.

It is crucial to maintain a situation where the consequences of business failure are appropriately limited. Do not personally guarantee leases or debt. Avoid borrowing money unless the lender understands it is high risk with equity characteristics (as with convertible debt). Team up with co-founders who truly understand the risks and are willing to take chances to find the right answers. Hire early employees who are comfortable with ambiguity and frequent changes of direction. Finally, bring on investors with a healthy respect for portfolio theory. Experienced early-stage investors expect failure in a meaningful portion of their portfolio and will not panic at your strategy changes.

With all this in place, you can experiment and learn as needed to create a major disruptive business, and as long as you execute competently, your *"gracious masters"* (including yourself) should be satisfied with the result.

For more on learning from hard knocks, see *Hitting Bottom* and *Wisdom from Experience*. For more on improving through learning, see *Surpassing*. For other approaches to gaining informatioon, see *Stepping Back* and *Maturity*.

A Narrative from Matt Munson
CEO AND CO-FOUNDER, TWENTY20

One of the most difficult periods in our company's history came only eight months into its life. The company's name at that time was Acceptly. Our first product aimed to make navigating college admissions easier for students via a free digital college admissions counselor. We'd raised $500k from a dozen angel investors as well as a leading education-focused venture capitalist, and we'd built a four-person team aimed at the education space. With our early product freshly launched, we earned a spot at a prominent startup accelerator.

The program was only twelve weeks long. Teams shared work space and attended daily sessions on different elements of business-building. The program was to culminate with a demo day where hundreds of investors would come to hear our pitches. Four weeks into the program, eight weeks from demo day, we realized we had a major problem on our hands. Aside from a few dozen excited users, no one was using our product. We'd now iterated through five different approaches to the problem, and nothing was working. During a Lean Startup-focused weekend course in Palo Alto, we walked around the mall talking to high school students about our idea. Their eyes glazed over. We realized quickly we'd utterly failed to understand our target user base before setting out to build a product and raise money. Moreover, after eight months of banging our heads against the wall trying to figure it out, we had a collective 'a-ha' moment: we realized we were also completely fed-up with the education space. We didn't want to do it anymore. But demo day was looming.

I'd be lying if I said I wasn't filled with anxiety. I was. And depression came knocking hard. I'd wake up at 2 AM most nights and lie awake for hours. This was my big shot at starting my own company. I'd spent most of my savings. In addition to my company being in crisis, I was expecting the birth of my first child the week after demo day! Those weeks were some of the hardest of my life.

All that said, as a team we had no time to panic. And we knew beating ourselves up because our early ideas failed wouldn't help. So we determined to go back to the drawing board. We started brainstorming other ideas we were excited about. Ultimately, we settled on the concept of enabling the Instagram generation to make money off their creativity by selling their photos to friends and followers as canvas wall art. We took the lessons we learned from Acceptly's failure to ensure we got those items right in our new product. We spoke early to hundreds of users and we tested our acquisition channels before we even built the first version of the product. The product took off out of the gates.

While we continued to make new mistakes, the muscle memory around how we responded as a team when Acceptly failed has served us ever since. When our initial photo product, Instacanvas, stalled out at around $1M in revenue, we pivoted yet again to enable our photographers to license digitally to major brands and agencies. That service, Twenty20, is now used by thousands of brands and is doing millions in revenue.

MILESTONES

"Not every end is the goal. The end of a melody is not its goal, and yet if a melody has not reached its end, it has also not reached its goal. A parable."

In other words: Getting to the end of something is not the same as getting to the goal of that thing. The goal of a melody is not simply to play to the end; nevertheless, if it has not played to the end, it has not reached its goal. This is a comparison to think about.

———————————

A common confusion in entrepreneurship is equating raising investment capital with success. Startup employees naturally see it this way, since their jobs, working conditions, and perceived status depend primarily on external financing in the short to medium term. The media exacerbate the confusion through the attention they give to venture capital investments. Raising a venture round is a great example of the distinction Nietzsche is making in this quote. The "*goal*" of raising capital is to provide operating fuel for the business so it can develop and grow. The *"end"* is marked by the wire transfer arriving in the company bank account. You must get to the end (receiving the money) to achieve the goal (growth), but they are not at all the same.

Nietzsche suggests that reaching the end is necessary, but not sufficient, to achieve a goal. In a business, achieving a particular milestone or end is often neither necessary nor sufficient. There are usually other routes to achieving the goal, and there is almost certainly more to do after reaching the milestone. Consequently, you should keep the actual goals in the back of your mind after developing and beginning to execute on a plan. You will construct milestones at a variety of levels of detail, but they are only means and measures and do not stand alone.

The distinction can be applied broadly. How do you weigh the ultimate goals for the company? Imagine that an acquirer pays a hefty sum for your company but dissolves it into their operations, and the industry disruption you had envisioned never really occurs. You definitely reached the end, but would you view that scenario as having achieved your goal? This is complicated by the fact that investors like to hear that you are aiming high, intending to build a large and influential business. You either already had that as your goal or you make it your goal. But the investor reality is that they are paid to return a multiple of capital to their own investors, not to disrupt industries. Their goal is a liquidity event. Companies that are in the process of succeeding at disruption often have liquidity opportunities, so the question arises in many successful firms. If the *"end"* of a liquidity event is not also your goal, you need to find a way to satisfy the investor's goal while continuing to pursue your own. This may mean being selective about acquisition scenarios or even aiming for an IPO.

You might also consider an even broader scope—your life and career. Perhaps selling your business is just a milestone on a larger path. There are many serial entrepreneurs. Elon Musk is a good illustration. He sold PayPal and became fabulously wealthy, but he clearly had bigger goals in mind. The sale of PayPal was a necessary end, and PayPal did indeed change how Internet payments are made. Yet, looking back from the perspective of his more recent career with Tesla and SpaceX (among other ventures), it was only an interim milestone in a larger arc—and is headed toward the status of a footnote. On the other hand, he may not have known any details of that larger arc. It may be that his goal was just to be fulfilled or to create a vision and will it into existence. Similarly, it is important to keep in mind that building a successful company might be just a milestone in the service of other life goals.

What are those goals for you? In many of the chapters in the section *Free Spirits*, we explore the notion of entrepreneurial success at the level of company, career, and life. If you have not thought about what success looks like and what your real goal is, then the difference between end and goal will come back to bite you. You risk reaching the end without reaching your goal.

For more on measurement, see *Stepping Back*. For more on the will to create your vision, see *Genius*. For more on staying focused on business success, see *Silent Killers*.

PLANNING

66 Making plans and conceiving projects involves
many agreeable sentiments. He that had the strength
to be nothing but a contriver of plans all his life
would be a happy man. But one must occasionally
have a rest from this activity by carrying a plan into
execution, and then comes anger and sobriety. 99

*In other words: Making plans and coming up with ideas is
fun. If you could afford to spend all your days just exploring
ideas, you'd be pretty happy. But once in a while you must
stop planning and coming up with ideas, and actually
implement them—which causes frustration and stress.*

We will end this section on *Strategy* by discussing the relationship
between planning and execution. Idea generation, strategy, and planning are a little like play—in a good sense. You have the opportunity
to fantasize about the future and think about how you might go about

realizing that future. In your fantasy, there are no nasty surprises, and while you know there are certain things you will need to deal with (competitors, customer resistance, distribution, and technical challenges), part of the fun is in figuring out how to handle those issues.

Things rarely go according to plan when you start to execute. It is impossible to know in advance all the factors that will arise during execution, and even if it were possible, conditions change in unpredictable ways.

There are two opposite ways to over-react to this problem. One is to avoid planning altogether, under the assumption that it is pointless. The other is to hold off on execution as long as possible and plan obsessively in the hopes of minimizing surprises.

Neither of these approaches is likely to work in a disruptive startup. The first will result in building the wrong business, the second in never building the right business. The solution to the dilemma is not to split the difference, but rather to engage in meta-strategy (strategy about strategy) and figure out how planning and execution should work together in your business.

The most obvious question to address is the cycle time, or rhythm, of planning and execution: how long do you execute on a plan before revisiting it? Typically the cycle will be faster in the early stages of the business than it is in a growth phase. In the earliest stages, every iteration of your minimum viable product could represent a pivot or strategic change. Your strategic horizon might be as short as days or a week. This is not unusual for companies in accelerator programs. Once you raise a large seed round of capital, the planning horizon becomes distinct from the product iteration cycle, and it should be at least one quarter in duration. This helps to avoid giving both the investors and your organization whiplash. It also gives your plans time to produce useful results and information. In a growth phase, you will need to plan a full year in advance so as to manage sales compensation, hiring, customer and partner expectations, and capital needs.

It could also make sense to have multiple planning and execution cycle frequencies, all operating in parallel and at different levels of the business. Raising a first financing round normally requires at least some planning over the full course of the capital runway, despite the expectation of pivots. A growth business with an annual plan needs to be able to respond mid-year to market shifts and external technology advances. Functional groups or smaller teams may achieve longer-term goals more effectively by emphasizing shorter time horizons and adjusting their plan each cycle.

Another aspect of your meta-strategy is how you will handle the inevitable "anger and sobriety" involved in execution. The plan, or some aspect of it, seems to be failing; what do you do? It may be that you include a faster-cycle evaluation process where you decide whether to continue with a plan or revise it. You may decide to have a general policy that you do not interrupt plans mid-stream, even if early results are discouraging, to counteract the natural human tendency to give up too soon. This can raise questions relating to the sort of culture you want to have. Do you and your team prefer a methodical approach to adaptation or a more opportunistic and event-driven style? Most important is to have some idea, in advance, how you will handle the elements that do not go as expected, even though you can't know specifically what they will be.

The details of how you go about strategic planning are also important to consider. Who will be involved? How is information gathered and organized? When in the cycle do you begin, and what are the stages of the process? How are the final decisions made, and how are they communicated to the organization? How often do you evaluate the strategic planning process itself, and what is the process of re-evaluation?

You will have noticed that we have provided some guidance but no definitive answers on your meta-strategy. We can't do this any more than we can tell you which markets to address or what product features you should develop. The meta-strategy you adopt and its own dynamics are specific to your business. You must both plan and execute, and to do that well, you should have a plan for how you will plan and execute.

For more on the complementary roles of vision and execution, see *Genius*. For more on entrepreneurship as play, see *Maturity as Play*. For more on obstacles that impede your plans, see *Overcoming Obstacles*. For more on the importance of looking at the business from the outside, see *Stepping Back*. For more on deciding whether to stick with a plan, see *Resolute Decisions*.

CULTURE

The opportunity to create a unique set of *cultural norms* for your company is one of the best parts of being an entrepreneur. Often, we simply call this *culture*, but there is an important distinction. View the cultural norms as the underlying rules and the culture as the instantiation of these rules through the selection and interactions of particular humans.

Nietzsche viewed his work as a bridge from the hegemonic culture of Europe to his own vision of a modern world. In doing so, he challenged existing cultural norms while inspiring many new ones.

In entrepreneurship, there is no singular approach to culture. Founders often entangle themselves in the "what" of culture, without thinking about "how" to define it or "why" it is important. Nietzsche gives us food for thought regarding both the how and the why, in addition to some abstract suggestions around the what.

Once again, read the Nietzsche quotes slowly while keeping in mind that he was a major influence on both Sigmund Freud and Carl Jung. Relish them as you consider how his thoughts in the late 19th century apply to contemporary entrepreneurship. Consider how you are implementing your cultural norms and whether any chapter inspires you to approach things differently.

TRUST

“ I am affected, not because you have deceived
me, but because I can no longer believe in you. ”

*In other words: I'm not upset that you lied to me. I'm upset
that I can never trust you again or think highly of you.*

Trust is the foundation of business relationships. It is an expectation
that someone will consistently follow a particular standard of behavior. Deception is a violation of that standard. While legal contracts can
prescribe some elements of a business relationship, it is impossible
for them to cover all contingencies. Even if it were possible, it is not a
motivating, positive way to operate.

In the early stages of any business relationship (whether with investors, suppliers, customers, or employees), you do not know the standards of behavior expected by the other party, and they do not know
yours. Ideally, such expectations would be communicated in advance,
but this rarely happens in a comprehensive way. Instead, people wait

until there is a perceived transgression to address these expectations. Experienced and rational businesspeople are not surprised or upset by these situations. As long as the behavior is not egregious, it will not be perceived as intentional deception.

Good working relationships are difficult to find. Trust and understanding grow over time. If you exhibit a reliable pattern, or the other party has explained their standards, they will come to expect consistency. This is when deeper deceit can occur. If you violate established standards or patterns after an extended relationship, the other person will see it as a genuine deception. They will no longer trust you and no longer believe in you. It is likely that they will react not by restoring you to newcomer status, but rather by no longer working with you at all.

The only hope for the future of such a relationship is if the deception was inadvertent and if you make amends absolutely and immediately. There are two actions you must take. First, apologize. Explain the assumptions under which you were operating, and show how you misunderstood the expectations of the working relationship. This must be sincere, and you must take complete responsibility. Don't say "you never told me..." but rather "I failed to recognize..." Second, you must do everything possible to make the other party whole. This may come at great personal cost to you in money or in reputation. In some cases, you cannot fully restore the situation. Then you have a continuing obligation to act in the interest of the other if you want to repair the relationship. Even so, it will take time. The initial deception will have felt like a ploy, and the person may, for a while, suspect these apologies and amends as a further ploy.

Such restitution is only possible because of what Nietzsche says here. If the person is upset about the deception itself, then there is no remedy because the deception has already occurred. But if she is upset because she can no longer believe in you, then it is at least possible to restore that belief by showing that you made an honest error that is unlikely to recur.

If the deception was not inadvertent, or you elect not to take these measures, then the end of that relationship may be only the beginning of your penance. People take different approaches to perceived mistreatment. Some will actively denounce you; others will only offer an opinion when asked. Regardless, someone who no longer believes in you will not keep it a secret, though they may use language couched in ambiguity, veiled suggestions, or noticeable omissions. Word will get out, and your reputation will suffer.

Nietzsche's quote hints at how you might manage the possibility of others violating your trust. You want to be in a position where you are only upset that you can no longer believe in them. One school of thought suggests that those who begin with trust are more successful because they are more open to positive relationships. They also learn better how to assess people because they are exploited in limited ways more often. Brad takes this position, relying on what he calls the "screw me once" rule. This does not mean that you give people, upon meeting them, the keys to your home and a signature card for your checking account. Instead, it indicates that you do not over-lawyer agreements and that you rely more on a positive working relationship than on procedural stipulations. You remain vulnerable while retaining stop-loss-type protections.

You must think through and experiment with how you manage trust—both how you offer it and how you earn it.

For more on earning trust, see *Gratitude and Integrity* and *Taking Responsibility*. For more on the variety of ethical standards, see *Monsters, Imitators,* and *Consequences*. For more on learning by taking risks, see *Wisdom from Experience*.

A Narrative from Ingrid Alongi
CO-FOUNDER, QUICK LEFT

In the months prior to the sale of my business, I found myself in an unfortunate situation. A person I had trusted, by default rather than through long experience, violated my trust. Luckily, I was alerted to these deceptions by people who respected me.

I had a difficult time figuring out how to deal with the situation. First, I had begun with high hopes that the working relationship with this person would be mutually beneficial. Second, I had made myself financially vulnerable through certain arrangements that exposed me personally. Third, the condition of the business was not ideal, with significant debt and volatile cash flow. To top it off, I was pregnant with twins. It is one thing to trust a new working relationship and be a little vulnerable. I was learning why it is important to limit that vulnerability.

I am a very competitive person. I had won multiple masters' track cycling titles while building this business from scratch! But now, I didn't have my usual competitive spark, because of the hormones and energy depletion related to the pregnancy and general burnout from starting a company. Further, I was very conscious of the fact that stress is not a good thing for a high-risk pregnancy. I simply didn't have the energy to figure out how to confront the situation and I felt an overwhelming sense of defeat.

I blamed myself for not seeing the warning signs earlier. Of course, behaviors that are obvious concerns in hindsight are difficult to read in advance. In our culture there is a personal/business boundary. As such, the saying, "it's not personal, it's just business" is taken by some people as license to act in a way that isn't always consistent with our notions of a trusting relationship. Further, the ability to manipulate people and situations to get deals done is considered an asset or a positive ability in business. The difference between these behaviors and dishonesty is often in the eye of the beholder. While it may be considered a skill to act this way, it's also a skill to be able to see through it, and to see how far it extends.

Once the dishonesty was revealed, I was truly in a lonely and isolated place. No one wanted to get involved at all, let alone volunteer to help. This isolation caused me to sometimes be in a state of denial of the dishonesty and to second-guess my instincts about the situation. As a woman, I faced further fears about speaking out – retaliation can be worse than just ignoring things and letting them go. I still wanted to believe in the person who had deceived me, and had exposed myself to enough risk that I was upset about the deception itself, due to its implications.

In the end, there was a positive outcome. I hired a personal lawyer and worked with a business coach to help make sure I wasn't second-guessing myself to inaction, or in this emotional maelstrom, over-reacting to elements that were not actually critical. I got through this difficult time: I gave birth to healthy twins, Quick Left was acquired, and no one lost their shirt or their house. Even better, I stayed with the company and we found ourselves in an almost unheard-of successful acquisition.

My biggest mistake was not insisting on crucial changes to the personal financial exposures I had prior to entering into the business arrangement. Things were moving quickly and (by design, as I later learned) pushing me to trust that the changes would get done in time, instead of insisting they get done before anything else moved forward. I let my excitement and optimism about the new arrangement and its potential cloud my judgment, setting myself up for a potentially dangerous situation later. As someone who likes to move fast, I learned yet again, that sometimes you need to slow down. If someone is pushing you to make a decision quickly, it's worth questioning why that is and whom it ultimately benefits.

GRATITUDE

"Whoever goes in new paths and has led many persons therein, discovers with astonishment how awkward and incompetent all of them are in the expression of their gratitude, and indeed how rarely gratitude is able even to express itself. It is always as if something comes into people's throats when their gratitude wants to speak, so that it only hems and haws, and becomes silent again."

In other words: Anyone who has been a creator and a leader has been surprised by how poorly people express gratitude, if they express it at all. It is as though the gratitude gets stuck in their throats and they can only say it half-heartedly before giving up.

As a leader, you know how important communication is to your success. You also know that your communication skills can always be improved. As Nietzsche observes here, gratitude is among the most difficult sentiments to effectively communicate. When a great CEO thanks customers or employees, it is unrushed, sincere, and memorable. Perhaps you already find this natural. If not, it is worth learning and practicing to overcome any awkwardness or resistance you have in genuinely expressing gratitude.

Imagine how powerful it would be for your company if the members of your team were more comfortable expressing gratitude. Employees who feel appreciated by others are less likely to engage in divisive behavior. Customers who feel valued will not be as tempted by your competitors. Vendors who feel acknowledged will go out of their way to perform. If you lead and teach your organization to express heartfelt gratitude, both within and without, it creates a substantial competitive advantage.

However, you cannot implement a culture of gratitude with a simple policy or script. Insincerely expressed gratitude is worse than none at all. Instead, address the underlying reason that it feels awkward to express genuine gratitude: it exposes *vulnerability*. When you thank someone truly, you are saying to them, "I wanted or needed something, and you provided it for me." Most people are not comfortable admitting this gap in their independence and autonomy. Before you can teach your organization to express gratitude, both you and they must first become comfortable with this vulnerability.

For more on the importance of gratitude and warmth, see *Gratitude and Integrity* and *Attracting Followers*. For more on the importance of emotion in communication, see *Once More with Feeling*.

A Narrative from Bart Lorang

CEO & CO-FOUNDER, FULLCONTACT AND CO-FOUNDER, VI.VC

It was 6:30 AM on a cold, snowy day in Boulder, and overnight it had dumped a foot of snow. To my surprise, when I awoke, my next door neighbor had already finished shoveling the snow from our sidewalk. My wife

Sarah needled me for allowing our neighbor to bear our burden. I tried to explain that I was busy with my CEO job, and that some things simply aren't priorities. That was the wrong answer: she openly wondered how our neighbor, also a startup CEO, had the time to shovel his walk and ours, even while his company was scaling faster than mine.

At that moment, I felt like a failure – as a CEO, as a husband, and as a man. I knew something had to change, and I needed help. So, after some consideration, I reached out to our lead investor to ask for an introduction to a widely recognized CEO coach, Jerry Colonna.

Make no mistake – for me, merely asking for help was a big deal. I grew up fiercely independent, never asking for help from anyone. Admitting to others that you need help is a way of showing vulnerability, and my Rocky Mountain upbringing and "rugged individualist" programming was completely counter to that type of exposure.

This simple request for help ultimately changed my life in a profound way. It connected me with Jerry, which enabled me to explore my past relationships, my approach to leadership, and examine some of the ways in which I had been complicit in creating unhealthy conditions at my company. It also helped me understand why we had created FullContact in the first place: to help people be more awesome with people.

I realized that we weren't living this credo at FullContact. Not even close. We had created a company culture that expressed itself through a deadly combination of machismo, passive aggressiveness, and a victim mentality.

So, I simply started modeling the behavior I had learned in coaching and sought at FullContact. We started by checking in personally at daily leadership meetings, using Red, Yellow, and Green to indicate where we all were personally. We asked the questions:

- *Where's our body?*

- *Where's our breathing?*
- *How are we doing, really?*

The culture shift began immediately. Members of our leadership team began bringing their whole selves to work. Leaders began to identify their fears, and to speak about them with their colleagues. Tears and hugs became the norm. Ad-hominem attacks and passive aggressive verbal jabs dissipated.

Amazingly, after our leadership team's transformation, our Board of Directors followed suit. I recall distinctly a Board meeting where tears were shed by a number of leadership team members, and Board members came forth with their own vulnerabilities. Our leadership team didn't feel threatened in this moment; rather they felt safe to share their deepest anxieties and fears.

Now, a few years later, we have transformed our entire culture into one in which love, vulnerability and gratitude thrive. For example, at every single All Hands on Deck meeting, we spend ten minutes expressing gratitude for one another and recognizing our colleagues. I now usually shed tears when I recognize a teammate each month for outstanding service. When we express gratitude in these ways, it is deeply sincere, because we arrived at this point by addressing the underlying discomfort with vulnerability. More generally and perhaps most importantly, our #1 core value of "Be Awesome With People" isn't just a tagline – it's now a principle by which everyone at FullContact tries to lead their lives.

PERSISTENCE

" It is not the strength, but the duration of
great sentiments that makes great men. "

*In other words: To achieve great success, strongly
held beliefs and motivations are less important than
consistently holding them over the long term.*

This aphorism highlights the distinction between duration and strength. Before considering that distinction, note that Nietzsche emphasizes "*great*" sentiments and men. He is probably not talking about avocational passions or the love of another person. Instead, he means sentiments that affect large numbers of people, long-established systems, and traditions, or that represent historically important ideas.

For you, this might mean disrupting a large, established industry. It could relate to a way of operating, such as taking a controversial ethical position or creating an organizational innovation. Using this interpretation, your great sentiment must incorporate a vision of the future. Otherwise, as the world changes—and today it changes faster than ever—it will lose relevance over time, implicitly limiting its duration.

To get started with your business, you need to believe intensely in your idea, your team, and your approach. Without the *"strength"* of your sentiment, no one will follow you, work with you, buy from you, or invest in you. A lukewarm leader is no leader at all. Consequently, it is easy to think that the strength of the sentiment is the key, or at least one key, to entrepreneurial success.

You cannot accomplish a great change or implement a great idea overnight. Though setting things in motion is essential, following through to the end is what turns initiative into accomplishment. Passionate "idea people" who merely get things started do not earn greatness; that requires carrying out the disruption. This can take a long time, and if you have a great sentiment, there will be much opposition obstinately standing in the way of your vision.

Sentiment that begins strongly may not last, because it can be depleted by constant naysaying. You may also get tired or bored. Not every person, and not every sentiment, can be sustained long-term. The daily grind of implementation does not look anything like your beautiful vision that drives and requires it. Other exciting ideas and opportunities will come along. The new Bright Shiny Object will tempt you, causing a decline in the strength of your original sentiment. The novelty and excitement of new sentiments may cut your interest short before greatness is realized.

Your strongly held sentiment can be lost, even if the business is doing well. Early success can breed sloppiness or neglect. Ego, financial freedom, or overconfidence can lead to fatal deviations from your original vision or sentiment. To be great, you must persist in a great sentiment until the result is great, not merely successful. At each stage, you must look for the next tier of achievement derived from the original sentiment.

The initial strength of a sentiment is not even a major determinant in how long it lasts. The duration required to produce greatness is longer than your initial enthusiasm can sustain. Instead, to outlast all of the barriers you face, the strength of your sentiment must grow despite the obstacles. Opposition and setbacks must produce enthusiasm rather than disappointment, intellectual curiosity must narrow rather than broaden, and success must produce renewed intensity. You must hold your sentiment deeply, not just strongly, to generate a cognitive bias producing entrenchment rather than revision. For your sentiment to last, it must be an obsession.

"What if the sentiment is wrong?" you might ask. In that case, it was never going to produce greatness. Duration of sentiment can also produce failure. While failing fast is a common entrepreneurial refrain, and sometimes it is appropriate, it also produces a habit of mind that excludes the kind of perseverance that greatness requires. By failing too fast or too frequently, you can be good or successful, but probably not great.

For more on obsession and its implications, see *Obsession*. For more on disruption taking place slowly, see *Patience in Disruption*. For thoughts on adapting your vision, see *Information*, *Milestones*, and *Planning*. For more on expressing the strength of beliefs, see *Strong Beliefs*.

A Narrative from Tim Miller

CEO, RALLY SOFTWARE

I don't consider myself a great man, so I am reluctant to write about this topic. Nevertheless, over the years I have managed to surround myself with great men and women who shared a vision, or "great sentiment," if you will. I can therefore humbly share a story about a great team by talking about my experiences as part of that team.

When I started my first company, Avitek, a central goal was to create a deeply-ingrained culture based on the Golden Rule – to treat other people the way we want to be treated. We achieved that goal, and bootstrapped a successful company. Still, most of the time we never had more than two to four weeks of payroll in our checking account. The risk of bankrupting my family weighed on me. When the opportunity arose to sell the company and gain financial freedom, I took it. Avitek was acquired at an attractive price just four years after its founding.

After a brief sabbatical, I joined my long-time business partner, Ryan Martens, who I have collaborated with my entire career, to help create Rally Software. During my time off, I had crystallized my desire to create an enduring company, one that would not only be successful, but would substantially change the software development industry. In particular, we aimed to unleash the creative genius of software developers by helping to ensure that they would be treated respectfully. This would in turn enable them to pursue the biggest opportunities in their markets and ultimately to help solve the biggest problems of the planet.

Our vehicle for achieving this vision was Agile software development. The Agile Manifesto is based on twelve principles, two of which capture the "great sentiment" that drove Rally:

- Give them (developers) the environment and support they need, and trust them to get the job done.
- The sponsors, developers, and users should be able to maintain a constant pace indefinitely.

This approach was in stark contrast to the command-and-control methods of "waterfall," prevalent in the first several decades of software *development. Those methods often resulted in "death march" projects that combined unsustainable levels of effort with unspecified duration. Such methods didn't scale to large teams solving large problems in innovative, game-changing ways.*

In order to build an enduring company, one of my first imperatives was to raise venture capital. We wanted to be a leader in our space, and would need to survive the challenges of disrupting an existing industry dominated by giants like IBM, HP and Microsoft. This would require considerable capital.

Venture capital indeed propelled us into a clear leadership position in our market, but after a decade of growth the need to return capital to our investors forced us down an IPO path. This ultimately made us susceptible to being acquired. Thus, raising venture capital both helped and hindered our ability to create a long-lasting independent company.

We had a terrific run for thirteen years. As a young public company we worked hard to "keep the band together" and to grow and remain independent. We continued to promote our "great sentiment," as Nietzsche puts it, our highest calling of saving the planet by changing the software industry. But we had some overwhelming obstacles to overcome. Increasingly our activist investors wanted board seats, with the goal of cutting back our investments in order to be more profitable. Although in the short run this might have made us more successful in the financial markets, there is little doubt that it would have also diminished our ability to pursue our mission. Unfortunately, we were not large enough and growing fast enough to survive the wrath of Wall Street, where quarterly profits are valued over long-term vision.

We ended up selling Rally to CA Technologies, a company that became great through acquisitions. They genuinely wanted to modernize their own processes to become Agile, and they valued our ability to help their customers win in the "application economy." The sale allowed Rally to continue its mission and thrive under the security of a multi-billion dollar umbrella. From day one, they treated people fairly, and every employee was either retained or assisted with finding a role in another division. While we didn't remain an independent company, I have no doubt that our mission continues to this day. We had a lasting impact on changing the software industry for the better, and I think the world is a better place because of technology our team built.

SURPASSING

66 Life herself spoke this secret to me: "Behold," said she, "I am that which must ever surpass itself." To be sure, you call it will to procreation, or impulse towards a goal, towards the higher, remoter, more manifold: but all that is one and the same secret. 99

In other words: Life is just a process of always surpassing oneself. You might think of this in the context of having children, of striving toward goals, of achieving something more, or something rare, or something with broad appeal. But all those are the same idea.

———————————————

The phrase "leveling up" originated with video games where one's skills are tightly matched to the progression of levels in the game. If you have the skills to succeed at a particular level, you move on to the next. Once you have those skills, you can consistently work your way through the prior levels and try again as often as you want.

Leveling up has currency in entrepreneurship. Applied to an individual or a team, it refers to improving the capabilities needed to meet an upcoming challenge of the business. For example, successfully supporting a million users is different from supporting ten thousand, and if your company is growing in that direction, your ops team must level up.

A related buzz-phrase is "continuous improvement." This is a more granular approach, where the individual or organization is always looking to make things better but is not necessarily aiming for particular targets. Under continuous improvement, an organization follows every endeavor with an effort to identify what was not done as well as it could have been and looks for ways to improve those things next time.

The idea of self-improvement is not new, but Nietzsche is saying something larger here. His idea is that improvement, or "*surpassing*," is what life consists of. Particular goals aside, one is always working to be better, broader, or fuller if one is truly living. Personal growth is not just one facet of life. It is life. You don't need to try to achieve more in a worldly sense. Rather, simply broaden and deepen your spiritual side.

You can apply the same idea to your business and its organization. At first glance, one might think that a business could achieve a certain revenue size with a certain profit margin and stabilize there. If its stakeholders are satisfied with the returns, products, and jobs, then what reason is there to change? But in a competitive and innovative market, there is no such thing as a stable situation. If you are profitable, someone will try to get a piece of that profit, or an innovation or cultural shift will eliminate the need for your product. The company and its organization must grow and improve just to maintain its status.

Leveling up, continuous improvement, or surpassing are not add-on or extracurricular activities. They are the essence of execution. Improving the team and the individuals who make it up is central to the strategy and operations of the business. If it is not, you will frequently be caught by surprise, suddenly realizing that you are behind in some area and need to do research, training, or unplanned hiring to come up to speed.

You need to plan for continuous and directed improvements in your organization. This requires similar intensity and consistency as you give to meeting your revenue targets. You cannot execute if your team does not have the necessary skills and knowledge. Those needs are always in flux, whether it is because your business is rapidly growing or the environment around you is changing.

For more on learning and growing through your business, see *Wisdom from Experience*, *Information*, and *Delight in Yourself*.

STYLE

"Culture is, before all things, the unity of artistic
style, in every expression of the life of a people.
Abundant knowledge and learning, however, are not
essential to it, nor are they a sign of its existence;
and, at a pinch, they might coexist much more
harmoniously with the very opposite of culture—
with barbarity: that is to say, with a complete lack
of style, or with a riotous jumble of all styles."

*In other words: Culture is first and foremost about the unity of
artistic style in every aspect of people's lives. Knowledge and learning
do not, by themselves, create culture and they are not essential to it.
Knowledge and learning might just as easily be found in an uncivilized
society with a complete lack of style, or many inconsistent styles.*

"Culture" developed its modern meaning in the 19th century as an outgrowth of the nascent field of anthropology. Application of the term

to business organizations began in the 1980s, and today many consider the analysis and active shaping of organizational culture a central aspect of successful entrepreneurship. While Nietzsche was referring to the culture of nations, his views also apply to business culture.

Is it reasonable to think of the employees of a company as *"a people"*? They undoubtedly spend more time together and have more interactions with each other than they do with their neighbors or other members of their geographic community. They have a degree of shared purpose that is rare among broader groups. They often have unique terminology and behavioral norms that bind them together while distinguishing them from individuals in other organizations.

"Artistic style" shows up in a business in a variety of ways. The best user interfaces, out-of-box experiences, product designs, and websites incorporate a strong artistic component. The interactions that employees have with customers, vendors, and the general public—in how they answer phones, in how they handle negotiations, and in the style of the Twitter feed—leave a distinctive emotional response. Development of the business as a whole is a creative endeavor that begins with an entrepreneur's vision expressed in a distinctive, concrete fashion.

Consider the cultural differences between Apple and IBM. Apple exhibits a clear unity of artistic style, and everything about their products, stores, advertising, and customer interactions exudes this style. This unity is also true of IBM, though the style itself is stodgy and uninspired.

Consider companies that do not have a unity of artistic style. What does their brand mean? What do you expect when you interact with them? What kinds of products will they offer in the future? If their culture consists of a *"jumble of all styles,"* something important is missing, even if the team members are smart, motivated, and collaborative.

In all your thinking about company culture, apply a lens of artistic style, and make sure that style is consistent and unified across all the company's activities.

For some subtleties regarding cultural unity, see *Groupthink* and *Right Messages*.

A Narrative from Tim Enwall
HEAD OF MISTY ROBOTICS

When I first read this quote and essay, I had a strong and negative reaction: in a business, culture *is what one hires for, promotes for and fires for and* brand *is what the public sees as the company's essence. A strong culture and a strong brand are crucial to success, and both must be built proactively, but they are distinct.*

I've long been a proponent of being very active in the development of company culture. Don't let it "grow organically," because that will result in that "riotous jumble of styles." People will work subliminally at cross-purposes, which radically impedes teamwork and success. Intentional brand image is driven by a small fraction of the company, and rarely do great brands let "just anybody" touch the image the public sees. Thus it's rare for a company to hire, promote and fire employees because "they're not luxurious enough for our luxury brand" or "not funny enough for our humorous brand". So, the notion that "culture is the unity of artistic style... of a people" was jolting and at odds with my world view.

Then I remembered the crisis at Google related to the public airing of a male employee's memo on their gender diversity efforts. This exposed the notion that despite our best efforts at separate brand building and culture building, the quintessence of the company shines through in myriad ways—imbued by both the internal culture and the external brand. This caused a deeper retrospective on my part into situations from my past.

What immediately popped to my mind was the "culture" of Nest—the company that bought Revolv, a company I helped build.

Nest was founded by Tony Fadell and Matt Rogers, both key members of the original iPhone team at Apple, and joined by a large cohort of ex-Apple people. I once worked at Apple and recalled it as having a highly combative culture where the smartest, loudest, brashest people were promoted. A company of supreme arrogance. And a wonderful culture of design ethic, customer centricity, and pride in engineering wizardry and perfection. Apple's ethos is dominated by the fact that they build hardware—which requires exactitude frequently enacted years before a product is in a customer's hands. A single hardware mistake, made 18 months before product debut, can have disastrous effects on the bottom line. One ex-Apple Nest employee related, "our saying at Apple was 'we polish the underside of the banisters'" Why? Because someone might look there, and that's high-quality perfection.

Along comes Google who plops down $3.2B to purchase Nest. They infused their new acquisition with cash and talent to propel it to greater heights. This included a large cohort of, now, ex-Googlers. Google's culture is built around Internet-connected software, with its instant billion-user marketplaces, rapid product iterations, "permanent beta" products, and "20% time" where engineers could spend a day-a-week on whatever software project they thought might lead to future Google success. The idea of locking down an aspect of the product 18 months in advance is as foreign to most Googlers as is the idea of inventing new features 3 weeks before product launch to most Nesters. This core dichotomy—"perfection" v. "adaptability"—caused untold subliminal strife. Most people couldn't put a finger on the cause; they just knew they were frustrated when "those crazy anal folks" (at Nest) spent vast hours and dozens of meetings on which exact plastic type to use for a connecting cable, or they were frustrated when "those fly-by-nighters (from Google) just tossed any old thing out to the market".

Because Google had bought Nest, many Googlers thought they were just transferring to another Google unit. Yet Nest was clear from day one that it would be "independently managed and operated." This, too, caused untold challenges. Googlers brought their accustomed hiring practices, corporate network assumptions, vendor choices, and budgetary habits to Nest. The Nest team chafed at the assumption that "of course" these practices would be adopted. Where was the independent creativity for "us as Nest to guide our own ship?".

This brings us back to Nietzsche's quote. At Google-Nest I saw up close and personal a "riotous jumble of styles.". Nest was "polished," Google was "fluid"; Nest "disciplined," Google "experimental"; Nest "premium," Google "ubiquitous." And so on. The travails of Nest after the acquisition are well-documented publicly in many press pieces. Many of these challenges can, in my opinion, be traced back to this disunity of artistic styles, which brazenly crossed that boundary between culture and brand.

Ultimately, the totality of these artistic styles (like it or not, brand marketers and human performance professionals!) is what a company's culture is. One style can't be hidden from the other; they ooze out of the pores of every nook and cranny of the business. All one needs to do is go back to review how Google's "brand perception" was affected by the public exposure of its "internal culture".

CONSEQUENCES

"The consequences of our actions seize us
by the forelock, very indifferent to the fact
that we have meanwhile 'reformed.'"

*In other words: We will have to face the consequences
of our actions, even if we have learned from our
mistakes and have corrected our behavior.*

While all of our actions have consequences, Nietzsche's phrasing suggests that his point is about actions involving questionable ethics. In business, the consequences of an ethical lapse rarely appear immediately. There is often a temptation to cut corners and deal with the cost later, perhaps with some hope that those negative consequences can be avoided altogether.

Views on what constitutes ethical business behavior vary widely. One entrepreneur will consider an activity just a common-sense tactic, while another will see that same activity as deceitful. Many executives define good and bad actions in terms of their effect on the business or the person taking the action. In most theories of moral development, this is analogous to the earliest stage, surpassed by most children around the end of elementary school.

There are forces driving convergence toward stricter standards. Customers, investors, and employees increasingly hold companies accountable for the ethics of their actions. The ethical domains being judged include factors related to the business, such as how it treats employees, as well as broader societal and environmental impacts. These judgments can also extend to vendors and their ethics. There can be negative consequences for firms that do not conform to broadly accepted business ethics.

Consider not just your own ethical judgment, but that of your customers and other stakeholders. Even if you believe that an ethical trend is ill-advised, you must take it into account or face the consequences. Follow the "*New York Times* Front Page Rule": don't do or say anything that you wouldn't want to see called out on the front page of the *Times*.

The second part of Nietzsche's quote says that when you take ethical shortcuts, it doesn't matter whether you stopped the offending behavior at some point, or even if it was only a single instance. It can still come back to bite you. Bad press is one way this happens. If you are caught having done something illegal, shady, or even just obnoxious, even if it was long ago, people will assume that you are still doing it or that you are doing other equally questionable things. Customers will lose respect for your brand, and you may no longer be able to hire the best employees. The proverb "where there's smoke, there's fire" often applies.

Your behavior also sets an example within the organization. Some employees are not thoughtful about their own ethical positions, and if they see that their leaders consider a behavior to be ethical, they will adopt that position. In a competitive organization, this can quickly evolve toward least-common-denominator behavior. If your initial lapse does not end up in the newspaper, eventually it will because the whole company acts that way.

The ethics of tomorrow may be the presiding judge for your actions of today. Just because no one calls out some behavior right now does not mean it will stay that way. If you only consider what is currently punished by the public, you will find yourself *"seized by the forelock"* for behaviors that pre-date the public outcry, even if you stopped when the new societal stance became clear.

Your only solution to this problem is to maintain high ethical standards independently of popular views. Happily, if you have evolved past the earliest stages of moral development, this is compatible with your approach. Resist the temptation to take ethical shortcuts, and pay attention to consensus ethical views as they evolve.

In his book *A Better Way to Think about Business: How Personal Integrity Leads to Corporate Success*, philosopher and Nietzsche scholar Robert Solomon described how building individual character in an organization can also help. This approach, which is called virtue ethics and follows Aristotle more than Nietzsche, complements the learning organization we describe in chapters like *Surpassing*, *Information*, and *Stepping Back*. Put ethics on your list of organizational measurement and improvement topics.

For more on ethical issues, see *Trust*, *Monsters*, *Taking Responsibility*, and *Imitators*.

MONSTERS

66 He who fights with monsters should be careful lest
he thereby become a monster. And if thou gaze long
into an abyss, the abyss will also gaze into thee. 99

*In other words: If your opponents are bad people there
is a risk that you will also become a bad person. If you
become too familiar with bad behavior it may start
to seem normal and infect your own thinking.*

Your moral compass is an important part of your identity. Similarly, company values are an important part of the identity and brand of your company. But there will be constant temptations to cut corners or make exceptions in the interest of expediency. You will often find yourself faced with a choice between upholding an abstract ethical principle and achieving a tangible positive outcome for the business.

Resisting these temptations becomes even more difficult when competitors, investors, employees, or customers do not share your standards. The problem is not that they break the rules but that they have different rules altogether. An investor might tell you that an action you consider wrong is not only perfectly acceptable but nearly mandatory, calling it "Sales 101." A competitor might use tactics that you consider underhanded, or that are illegal, to win business. A customer might use your transparency and forthrightness against you in a contract renewal negotiation.

There is nothing wrong with reconsidering your values and how they are applied. Perhaps you erred on the side of idealism with noble but unrealistic intentions. But do this on a principled basis, just as you did when you first detailed your company values. Do not rationalize or excuse behavior you still consider wrong. Lowering ethical standards is a one-way, downhill street. Once a class of behavior is considered acceptable in your organization, it requires a major effort to remove it.

"The abyss" consists of those companies who have achieved commercial success despite what you consider unethical, corrupt, or illegal behavior. You want that success, and you see that it has worked for them. You find yourself drawn to the potential benefits of this unethical, corrupt, or illegal behavior. Only you can decide where to draw your lines, but the only defense against the abyss is vigilance.

For more on issues with an ethical dimension, see *Trust, Imitators,* and *Consequences.* The monster can also be your own ego: see *Taking Responsibility.*

A Narrative from the Co-Founder of an Entertainment Software Company

After we unveiled our flagship product, which was universally acclaimed as the best in the market category, our direct competitor started behaving very badly. They bad-mouthed us and our product all over the place; they lied to our suppliers (content licensors) and to our retail customers ("we happen to know that they will never ship their product on time"). They lied to press and consumers, and they tried to strong-arm the platform owners into anti-competitive policies. They refused to pay royalties they clearly owed us (from use of our intellectual property in their own product), so we had to sue them for it. And then they lied in court like it was going out of style.

I recall there was ample frustration at the time about the fact that, by walking the upright path, we were fighting with one arm tied behind our back. But there was never a conversation along the lines of "maybe we need to start lying and saying bad things about them, too." We just sort of had faith that by being honest and transparent with our audience and other constituents—and polite and respectful vis-à-vis our competitors—that everything would work out in the end. I wouldn't even say that this was a "strategy choice," so much as what just felt right and natural.

GROUPTHINK

> " Insanity in individuals is something rare—but in groups, parties, nations, and epochs it is the rule. "

In other words: People generally act rationally on their own, but when they get together in organized groups they become irrational.

Alignment is crucial to organizational success. Members of a team must work toward the same goals; otherwise, individual efforts cancel each other out. However, there is a common confusion that alignment is the same thing as agreement. This is incorrect: alignment is about action, while agreement is about beliefs and opinions. Alignment means that everyone agrees on what the company is doing but not necessarily what it should do. Nevertheless, it is much easier to achieve alignment when there is agreement.

Your company becomes an echo chamber when you fail to distinguish between alignment and agreement. You will hire people who agree with your views, and candidates who agree with those views will self-select. You will apply charisma to reinforce your views. When a critical mass of homogeneity is reached, social pressures will crowd out non-consensus views. The result is groupthink, a term coined to have intentional echoes of George Orwell's *1984*.

Some people view this as a pleasant and productive state of affairs. Alignment is now a simple matter. Eliminating dissent reduces drama, keeps people focused on their jobs instead of debate and politicking, and makes it easier to present a united front to the world of customers and investors. Without much additional effort, you can develop a consistent cultural style. So what is the problem?

The problem is that your views are almost certainly wrong. Business is an environment of imperfect information where hypotheses are difficult to test reliably. Epistemic humility is required: the likelihood that your actual views are exactly correct is low, and there is only a moderate chance that they are mostly correct. But even if your views are mostly correct, this will only be the case at a particular moment in time. The world, your market, and your products are constantly changing. Today's correct views are tomorrow's errors.

A groupthink environment acts like a coiled spring or a gyroscope. Any attempt to change its direction is opposed by strong forces that bring it back to its original position. You will have built an organization that is perfectly tuned to pursue a single, incorrect direction. When you learn more or the market shifts, the inertia of groupthink resists the new information.

Nietzsche helps us see how easy it is for this to happen. It is *"insanity"* because the consensus view is dictated by history and social pressures, not by reason and reality. Furthermore, people tend to become zealous when everyone around them holds the same views. Alan Greenspan called the dotcom stock market "irrational exuberance." From up close, it made perfect sense (or fit with other agendas), but when considered objectively from a distance, it looked like insanity. The tendency for groups and organizations to converge on a consistent set of opinions is a natural outcome of having a group in the first place. To avoid this, it must be actively opposed.

Opposing the tendency toward groupthink requires that you build a different kind of culture, which takes considerably more effort to manage and lead. The organization needs to stay aligned while sustaining a certain level of disagreement. Team members need to wholeheartedly execute on a decision while simultaneously disagreeing with it.

Employees, especially leaders, with this inclination and ability can be difficult to find. Look for people who played team sports in high school or college. Military veterans strongly understand this principle. In contrast, you should avoid hiring anyone who exhibits passive-aggressive tendencies.

You can develop and reinforce a culture of alignment that allows for dissent. Before a decision is made, encourage a large variety of opinions. After the decision is made, any disagreements must be diminished, and everyone should get to work with the decision as their guide. This idea, along with the distinction between alignment and agreement, can be taught to the organization. Compensation, promotion, and terminations play a role in reinforcing the appropriate behavior. When someone strongly disagrees, showing appreciation for their cooperation and future alignment is essential.

It is easy to determine whether you have created a groupthink culture. When consensus is easy to reach or many decisions are unanimous, groupthink is likely present. Recent organizational research, using Bayesian analysis, showed that with only a 1% prior probability of systematic bias, a group of ten people all agreeing brings the probability of such bias to about 50%. If you aren't always a little bit frustrated by the dissenting opinions in the organization, you probably have some groupthink happening.

For more on team members who can execute on a decision without necessarily agreeing, see *Independence of Mind* and *Integrators*. For a deeper discussion of the sharp boundary between the pre- and post-decision periods, see *Resolute Decisions*.

INDEPENDENCE
OF MIND

"What shall I do with these two youths! ...they are unwelcome disciples to me. One of them cannot say 'Nay,' and the other says 'Half and half' to everything. Provided they grasped my doctrine, the former would suffer too much, for my mode of thinking requires a martial soul, willingness to cause pain, delight in denying, and a hard skin,—he would succumb by open wounds and internal injuries. And the other will choose the mediocre in everything he represents, and thus make a mediocrity of the whole,— I should like my enemy to have such a disciple."

In other words: I don't want these two young people as my followers. One of them always agrees and the other is indecisive. If they understood how I approach things, the first would find it painful and would fail, because my thinking requires combativeness, a willingness to cause others discomfort,

delight in saying no, and a tough skin. The other would
always opt for mediocrity and would drag down everyone
else. I wish people like that would work for my enemies.

In deciding what kind of people you will surround yourself with, you might consider many dimensions, including their motivational structure, cultural style, skills, and perspective. Here we will address their independence of mind.

It is not necessary to have a *"martial soul"*—an inclination toward conflict—to despise a "yes-person." If you are a confident leader, you see yourself as someone who is not afraid to be challenged. You can hold your own in a debate and are willing to change your mind without embarrassment if someone proposes a superior idea. People who always agree with you, therefore, add nothing.

The distinguishing behaviors and causes are not always obvious. Many individuals pick their battles to give them leverage in areas that matter most to them. This is strategically sensible for them, but it means that on many matters, you are receiving unhelpful deference. Other people are more manipulative, arguing with you just up to a point and then conceding, gaining your favor by both seeming to be independent but also not making waves. You can fall into your own trap, stating publicly that you welcome dissent but subtly favoring those who are more inclined to agree. Sometimes you will tire of the dissent and simply want to move forward.

As Nietzsche alludes, such people do not add much value and can detract from execution. They might find it difficult to maintain a strong position, when needed, with customers, vendors, and employees. Despite their apparent alignment with your direction, they will end up bending in other directions. Both you and your business end up suffering.

The consummate compromiser cannot hold a line. This person's agenda is to avoid both confrontation and genuine cooperation. This can be passive-aggressive behavior or it can be indecision and unwillingness to commit. Regardless, it provides little contribution to your thought process since there is no attempt to find better solutions, only to avoid arguing or fully supporting you.

Nietzsche does not address a third category: the perennial naysayer. Instead of always agreeing, this person always has reasons why objectives are impossible to achieve and approaches cannot possibly work. This might be due to a fear of commitment or of failure. In some cases, it is the "yes-person" turned on its organizational head: some managers cannot say "no" to their staff, who are often seeking to make their own jobs less stressful. The result is underperformance through sandbagging.

People with true independence of mind do not have a standard response and do not play games with their point of view. They express it, fight for it if they have high confidence in their view, and respect healthy debate in the limited-information context of business. This takes on a variety of styles, ranging from passionate advocacy to a neutral, intellectual tone. One can trust them to say what they think.

Independence of mind cannot stand alone. People need to know when to disagree privately instead of publicly. They need to be willing to accept and affirm a decision that goes against their views and implement it as if it were their own. Independence of mind does not mean undermining the alignment of the business. Rather, it means using the best of one's abilities to help determine and implement the alignment.

For more on alignment, see *Groupthink* and *Right Messages*. For additional angles on having a variety of leaders in your organization, see *Two Types of Leaders*, *Integrators*, *Faith*, *Deviance*, and *Introverts*.

A narrative from Gary LaFever and Ted Myerson
CO-FOUNDERS, FTEN AND ANONOS

In our experience, people who exhibit independence of mind help us inno-vate, while "Yes Men" leave us with no more knowledge than we had when we first shared a thought. This also applies to people outside the orga-nization, such as vendors and customers. In such cases, a key variable is engagement. Those who do not wish to engage will provide an "Easy No" or a "Grin Fake" depending on which best serves their purposes. Those who engage, in contrast, offer a "True Yes" or an "Invested No," based on their genuine assessment. Our examples come from the two companies we have started together.

FTEN

After direct electronic market access became well-established in the 1990s, myriad trading platforms connected to multiple financial markets around the globe. While each trading platform included self-contained risk man-agement capabilities, none provided cross-system or cross-exchange risk management. When we asked experienced financial market engineers why only vertical risk management was in place, instead of cross-exchange and cross-system risk management, we were told "it is just not done that way on Wall Street." The answer was an "Easy No." When we asked Colorado Front Range engineers who "didn't know better" the same question, they built our cross-exchange/cross-system risk management system. Their response was a "True Yes." Once the new risk-management system was completed, it had to cover all markets to be effective. But when we asked the New York Stock Exchange (NYSE) if they supported the real-time elec-tronic drop copies we needed as input to our system, they replied with an "Easy No." Only after we discovered that, unlike the rest of the industry, the NYSE called electronic drop copies "clearing copies" and re-asked the question, using their vernacular, did we get the "True Yes" we needed for our system. We had to speak NYSE's language to garner engagement and overcome their "Easy No."

When competitive providers started to enter the market, we asked customers if these solutions met their needs. They frequently said "Yes," but what they meant was that having those other solutions provided them with a "check the box" solution. They were just good enough to avoid or minimize fines if a regulator happened along. They did not want to engage with deeper risk management considerations, so these responses were "Grin Fakes."

ANONOS

Our founding thesis at ANONOS was that increasing risks from using data containing sensitive, restricted or legally protected information posed risks that would benefit from enhanced, granular-level privacy and security controls. We traveled the globe and met with chief privacy officers, security experts, legislators, regulators, and white-hat hackers. We asked if technically enforced controls existed that met their regulatory objectives and provided adequate risk protection. We received well-reasoned "Invested No's" from these advisors, and their input enabled the successful design, development and deployment of an entirely new approach to data risk management.

Once we had developed this innovation, we shared it with the chief privacy officer of a Fortune 100 company. She was quite familiar with the upcoming regulations and penalties in the EU, so when she responded positively we were able to take it as a "True Yes" due to her engagement.

We have the highest regard for people who are willing to provide "Invested No's" and an occasional "True Yes" to questions and ideas. We actively seek them out to work with because they help to make transformative innovation possible.

MATURITY

"He who acquires merit early in life tends to forget all reverence for age and old people, and accordingly, greatly to his disadvantage, excludes himself from the society of the mature, those who confer maturity. Thus in spite of his early merit he remains green, importunate, and boyish longer than others."

In other words: Those who are successful at a young age tend not to appreciate and respect older people. As a result, they do not spend time with those who have experience and maturity. This puts them at a disadvantage because, despite their early success, they remain novices and immature.

"Young people are just smarter," said Facebook founder Mark Zuckerberg at a 2007 venture capital conference. As of 2016, the median employee age at Facebook was twenty-eight. It seems that Nietzsche's point is still potentially relevant.

Yet this view did not stop Zuckerberg from tapping the wisdom of mentors many years his senior. Early on, he developed a relationship with *Washington Post* CEO Donald Graham. Later, he and Steve Jobs became close. Early Facebook investor Roger McNamee was a key mentor. Zuckerberg clearly understood the value of wisdom, at least in selecting his personal advisors.

While it is debatable (and controversial) how widespread Zuckerberg's expressed attitude is, if you are a younger entrepreneur, be careful not to fall into the trap of thinking that older people have nothing to offer. It is easy to be dismissive of the value of wisdom and experience, in contrast with youthful exuberance and dynamism. Our gut instinct for "cultural fit" responds to similarity along many dimensions, some of which—including age—can be detrimental. This warning applies not only to your selection of mentors and advisors, but also to identifying co-founders and management team members, as well as your entire organizational approach to hiring.

A mutually caring relationship with an older mentor can transform you from a whiz kid, who moves fast but burns up a lot of money and energy reinventing mistakes, into a superb entrepreneur, who often seems wise beyond her years. This is because many rookie errors are timeless, and the range of such mistakes that a wizened mentor has encountered, and can help you mitigate, is large.

In addition to helping with business decisions, an experienced mentor can help you handle your own emotional reactions to circumstances. The first time you experience the gut-wrenching fallout from a failed customer implementation, a public relations disaster, a lawsuit, or the loss of a key employee, it might seem like the end of the world. An older mentor who has been through these situations many times can offer empathy as well as help you stay calm, focused, and rational.

If you are early in your company's journey, you may be seeking co-founders. Consider teaming up with someone older. Recent studies suggest that, on average and despite outliers, companies started by middle-aged entrepreneurs have a better track record. One causal explanation for this statistic is the benefit of domain knowledge. A key to success in many technology areas is a deep understanding of industry structure. The barriers to entry in an industry are often less about capital, brand, or features, and more about knowing how people in the industry think, how and where they buy the sort of product you are offering, and which issues matter. Domain knowledge takes a long time to accumulate and usually involves both relationships and experiences. Experienced individuals with connections and domain knowledge can help you find the seam in the market to not only achieve product/market fit but also devise a go-to-market strategy that will work in that particular industry.

At later stages of a company's progress, a similar logic applies to hiring executives and managers. You probably realize that a little gray hair in the CFO chair brings comfort to investors. But it can also be valuable in sales and marketing roles. For many businesses, paying customers are middle-aged or older. If you are selling to large organizations, these are the influencers and decision-makers. Yes, you may have a champion in the customer organization who is younger, but this alone does not close the sale. Having an experienced hand at your side brings comfort to customers and enables you to anticipate their concerns. If you are selling to consumers, older people, on average, have considerably more disposable income than younger people. Even if your actual users are younger, their parents may be paying the bill. Insight into how these consumers think and behave is crucial. It is much easier for a member of a specific demographic to interpret data and know what data to collect about that demographic.

Finally, make sure that your broader hiring processes and attitudes do not dismiss older candidates prematurely. The most obvious reason is that you can miss out on great employees who just happen to be older. Another is that, due to employing generally less experienced people, your business will waste time developing tactics and strategies *de novo* when easy, tried-and-true methods already exist. It can also shortchange your startup by creating a particular form of groupthink. People at different stages of life often have different ways of thinking about things along with different priorities. The interplay of these different ways of thinking can help propel your business to success.

For some examples of the sort of rookie errors that experienced mentors, co-founders, and managers can help with, see *Patience in Disruption*, *My Way*, and *Groupthink*. For more on the benefits of domain knowledge, see *Doing the Obvious*.

A Narrative from Brad Feld

CO-FOUNDER AND PARTNER, FOUNDRY GROUP

After eighty-nine years on this planet, Len Fassler passed away at the end of the first week of 2021.

Len was my Yoda. As a paternal figure, he was a close second to my father. I loved him deeply. And I will miss him every day.

In the spring of 1993, Jim Galvin, CEO of Allcom, introduced me to Len. Allcom had just been acquired by Len's company, Sage Alerting Systems, and Len asked Jim who else he should talk to in the Boston area. Feld Technologies worked with Allcom whenever we needed a network installed for a client, so Jim introduced us, and that led to lunch near our office in downtown Boston.

Soon after, Len called me and asked if I'd have an interest in selling Feld Technologies to Sage Alerting. Dave and I took a while to decide to do it, but we closed the sale in November 1993.

Len and I ended up working together on many things over the past twenty-seven years. I still have the Brooks Brothers striped shirt that Len and his partner, Jerry Poch, gave me when we signed the documents for Feld Technologies to be bought by Sage Alerting Systems (which changed its name to AmeriData). When I started making angel investments in 1994, Len invested alongside me in many companies, including NetGenesis, Harmonix, and Oblong. We then co-founded Sage Networks (which changed its name to Interliant) with two other partners. As a partner at Mobius Venture Capital, I invested in Vytek, another company Len co-founded. As an angel, I personally invested in Core BTS, the company Len co-founded after Vytek was acquired.

Going for a walk was a foundation of our relationship. Whenever we were in the same office, I knew we had something to figure out if Len came by my desk and said, "Brad, let's go for a walk." When we weren't together, the phone call was the metaphorical equivalent of a walk. He had a remarkable talent for bringing up issues directly yet clearly and working through them quickly.

Everything I learned about buying a company, selling a company, or doing a deal came from Len. If you've ever worked with me in any deal capacity, I'm channeling Len. I learned how to be a board member from Len. I learned how to complete a negotiation, walk away from the table, be empathetic, and be available. He also taught me how to move on when something didn't work out or go my way.

I remember sitting at the Interliant office in New York after the IPO roadshow, waiting for the SEC to clear our filing so we could price. We were waiting for one document, after which we'd sign one more thing, and the bankers would price the offering, and we'd go public the next morning. When the fax machine printed ten pages (instead of two) that were additional comments on our SEC filing (that same one about which Merrill Lynch had said three weeks earlier, "we are good to go on the *roadshow—the SEC always clears this on time"), we knew we weren't pricing that night. Our order book collapsed two days later. We went public two months later, but we drank a lot of Scotch that night.*

I remember a phone call on December 1, 2000, when Len called me from New York. He told me that Cable & Wireless wasn't moving forward with the acquisition of Interliant—the deal was all but done. Rather than approving the deal, the C&W board decided to stop all M&A activity given they just found out they would have their first quarterly loss in many years. That night, Len joined about fifty friends at the Greenbriar Inn in Boulder for my surprise 35th birthday party, which Amy had arranged. He had a remarkable ability to take every setback in stride.

I remember the day before Fitbit went public in June 2015, I had breakfast with Len at the Gramercy Park Hotel, where I was staying. I told him I had the morning off and asked him what he wanted to do. He said he'd never been in Gramercy Park, since it was a private park, so we got the key to the park from the concierge and walked around it and talked for an hour. We then wandered around the Baruch College buildings talking some more. We ended that morning with a big hug like we started and ended all of our days together.

I loved the way Len put his arm around me. I loved the hug he always gave me. I loved how we said "I love you" when we said goodbye in person or on the phone.

Len changed my life. He gave me my second-favorite quote, "They can't kill you and they can't eat you" (my dad gave me my first-favorite quote, "If you aren't standing on the edge, you are taking up too much space").

If you've ever heard me say, "Would you buy it for a dollar?" I learned that from Len. His influence on me formed the basis of my business philosophy, now called #GiveFirst. He was one of the first lawyer-turned-entrepreneurs I worked with, which helped me appreciate the importance of law in business and the importance of business judgment in the law.

Len's ultimate brilliance was his ability to build deep emotional and enduring relationships and to "confer maturity" through those relationships. The number of people he influenced and who loved him is extraordinary.

INTEGRATORS

"The Most Necessary Apostle.—Among twelve
apostles one must always be hard as stone, in order
that upon him the new church may be built. "

*In other words: Among one's immediate followers, who
are leaders in turn, the most necessary is the one who is
tough and unwavering, so that the goal can be achieved.*

The best management teams include a variety of personality types and styles. This may seem counterintuitive—it is much easier to work with people who see things the same way that you do, as alignment is one goal of leadership. But alignment and agreement are different things. A healthy push and pull within the management team is important to ensure that it does not become an echo chamber. Otherwise, you will make unbalanced decisions that miss the complexity and nuance of your business environment.

Some people are idea generators, opportunity seekers, and perceivers of possibility. They are inclined to say yes to things, to give people the benefit of the doubt, to inspire, to be optimistic, and to focus on the upside. Others are *"hard as stone"*: they filter ideas, mitigate risks, say no frequently, hold people accountable, and prefer contracts to casual arrangements. In their book *Rocket Fuel*, Gino Wickman and Mark Winters call these two roles "Visionary" and "Integrator," respectively, and suggest including both types on the company's leadership team. Either type can be a founder or a CEO. A CFO or VP of Engineering is often an Integrator. A VP of Sales is usually a Visionary. If a company has a COO, that person and the CEO are often, perhaps preferably, of the opposite type.

Do not take this to mean that you are aiming for a team that is polarized in its inclinations. Instead, the best people have preferences in different directions and work toward being just a little less that way. If they start out entirely polarized, they need to "level up" and learn how to see things another way. This growth is not to change their role, but rather to make it possible for the team to work together toward superior decisions and aligned action.

If you are not a person who is hard as stone, make sure you have someone on the team who is. Learn to appreciate that person and how she is laying a foundation for the *"church"* you are trying to build. Teach her how to propose alternatives rather than simply to say no. Encourage her to listen to ideas before discounting them too quickly. Show appreciation when you realize she has saved you from yourself.

If you are hard as stone, you probably agree strongly with Nietzsche. If so, challenge yourself to get the others to believe and value it. There have been some highly visible startup successes where the infrastructure never got built and chaos ruled the day—until the company was bought for a vast sum. As a result, some people have concluded that it is not necessary to take care of the uninspiring hygiene factors of a business. Instead of accepting this, identify companies with great ideas that failed because they did not have this balance. There are *far more* companies like this, but they are harder to find because they no longer exist and are rarely well-known. Still, the examples are out there.

The person who is hard as stone does not create opportunities. Instead, she ensures that company leadership thinks through important decisions instead of making them rashly. She insists that the genuine constraints of the company are respected. She makes sure that your seizing of those opportunities will actually *work*. At least one of the company's "*apostles*," the members of your management team, must think that way.

For more on the difference between alignment and agreement, see *Groupthink* and *Right Messages*. For ideas on how to move the organization past entrenched polarization, see *Surpassing*. For more on the benefits of an Integrator, see *Cleaning Up*.

FREE SPIRITS

For Nietzsche, the best human beings are what he calls *free spirits*. Early in *Thus Spoke Zarathustra*, a section called "The Three Metamorphoses" describes three stages a free spirit must pass through in its full development: the camel, the lion, and the child.

The camel is a dutiful beast of burden, in a humble but not humiliating way. It is virtuous and willing to bear any difficulty to accomplish what is needed. But the camel is isolated from those who choose the comfortable and easy, leaving its spirit in a *"desert."* In this desert, the camel transforms into the lion, which actively opposes tradition, taboos, and the status quo. In particular, the lion responds to the *"Thou Shalt"* of the world with a *"Holy No."* The lion is a contrarian, an isolated iconoclast. But a spirit cannot create new values simply by saying "no" to the ways of the world. For that, it must become the child, which has a beginner's mind and sees the world as play, as a fresh start, as perpetual motion. The child speaks a *"Holy Yes,"* which enables it to dictate its own will, not in reaction to the world but independently. As spiritualist Ken Wilber puts it, these transformations do not each supersede the preceding stage, but rather they "transcend and include."

It is not hard to see how this maps onto disruptive entrepreneurship. The camel gets things done but is too embedded in the tasks of the moment to produce more than incremental change. The lion sees what is broken in the world and refuses to just go along but has no way to find a truly novel path. The child frees itself of its attachments and starts fresh, enabling it to create an entirely new way of doing things that shakes an industry to its foundations.

While not a perfect match, the philosophy of Stoicism is similar to the camel stage. It is a crucial first step for an entrepreneur because, above all, an entrepreneur must be willing to do the hard work and manage the inevitable psychological blows. It is valuable for operating a small business or consultancy, or for working as an employee in a high-growth startup. But if you have larger ambitions—if you want to create a large and important company—you will need to go beyond being the camel.

Nietzsche makes another distinction that positions his approach relative to Stoicism: the Apollonian and the Dionysian, based on the Greek gods Apollo and Dionysus. For Nietzsche, Apollo represents the dispassionate, rational, conceptual, and methodical side of a person. Dionysus represents the passionate, carefree, social, and ecstatic side. Nietzsche saw the post-Enlightenment world as out of balance with respect to these two sides and promoted the Dionysian as an antidote to what ailed society. This does not mean that he thought one should abandon the Apollonian entirely and live as a raving lunatic. Rather, he saw the mix as unbalanced. The Apollonian has much in common with Stoicism through eschewing the passions in favor of rational and dedicated effort. Like the camel, it gets things done, but there is something crucial missing.

How you relate to each chapter will depend on whether you are currently a camel, a lion, or a child. If you want to stretch yourself, read each chapter once with the mindset first of a camel, then of a lion, and finally of a child. Consider how you might approach your current situation differently using each perspective.

DEVIANCE

" Deviating natures are of the utmost importance
wherever there is to be progress. "

*In other words: Progress requires people who are naturally
inclined to do things differently from everyone else.*

Creating a large and important business usually requires making dramatic and disruptive improvements, not just incremental changes. What kind of people create disruptive change? They are people who do not feel pressure to conform the way most do. They do not think outside the box; they wonder "what box?" They don't just have good ideas; they see things from an entirely different angle. To others, their ideas often seem crazy. One might say they have a *"deviating nature."*

Unusual and visionary thinking is a necessary but not a sufficient condition for disruption and success. Many nonconformists have unusual yet unhelpful ideas. Even those who are successful probably have more bad crazy ideas than good ones. There is no reliable way to know in advance which people have good crazy ideas or which crazy ideas are good. The only way to know is to test them.

An important feature of a deviating nature is not just holding or talking about unusual ideas, but being willing to put those ideas into action. If you do not have a deviating nature and someone else in your company does, you must help choose among these ideas and put them to the test. This is one of the reasons why testing and learning is so important in a startup.

People who see things differently in their business tend to have a *"deviating nature"* in other areas of life as well. They might be social misfits, generally rebellious, mistrustful of authority, or have difficulty articulating their ideas. This is a continuum where one can create brilliant innovations without also being a pariah. However, there are bound to be at least some quirks and behaviors that the PR and HR departments would rather were not present.

Like anything else in your business, this should be managed. The business needs to get the benefit of visionary ideas without suffering from these quirks or rebellious behavior. If you are the person with a deviating nature, consider bringing on partners or staff who can buffer the world and the company from the most detrimental of your predilections. In addition to being more successful, you will probably also be happier. If someone else on your team has a valuable deviating nature, isolate their job responsibilities and organize their interactions in a similar fashion. The goal is to enable and facilitate their creative thinking to disrupt the world but not to disrupt the normal operation of your company.

For more on the importance of making large rather than incremental improvements, see *Domination*. For more on managing the scope of disruption, see *My Way*. For more on the role of a founder with a deviating nature, see *Two Types of Leaders*. For more on what it means to have both a vision and a drive to see it through, see *Genius*.

A Narrative from Luke Kanies
FOUNDER OF CLICKETY AND PUPPET

They say that if you're playing poker and, looking around the table, you don't know who the sucker is, it's you. When I started Puppet, it was me.

For years I attended the annual LISA conference, a community organized around the tools and practices of system administration. The membership ranged from people who maintained a couple of machines for a school to those who managed a gigantic infrastructure in corporate or research environments. I was initially overjoyed to find other people doing the same job as me, but I quickly grew cynical. The sysadmins around me were so focused on the minutiae of their work that they didn't realize how much better it could be. They were content with what they had, while I had sought this community specifically because I wanted help changing things.

I found a smaller group, more aligned with my goals. Their belief in the need for automation separated them from the rest of the conference. Everyone in this circle was building their own tools, trying to reframe the job of the sysadmin. I joined a community within a community, a clique within a crowd. This was where I belonged.

Or so I thought.

I soon grew frustrated again. What actually drew this group together was an intellectual pursuit, the desire to prove something in the abstract. There was no interest in putting their beliefs to the test. They were perfectly content to sit in a darkened room arguing indefinitely about whose tool was "better."

I learned a lot in those conversations, but overall I was disgusted. When I looked around the broader conference, I saw people who needed help. Their jobs were mostly repetitive, tedious work, punctuated by emergencies.

Executives would swoop in, blame the sysadmins, and then storm off without empowering them to fix any of the core problems.

This little group I was in wasn't going to argue its way into changing the world. Someone had to do something. Someone had to turn these intellectual experiments into a product that everyone could use. But building it wasn't enough: I knew by then that it takes a lot of work to get the market to adopt new technology. It needs a sales team, marketing, services people to help get it set up.

One of us was going to have to start a company.

It obviously wasn't going to be me. Everyone else in the room already had production software. They had working tech. Most of them had PhDs, and had been thinking about this problem longer than I'd had a computer. I set in to wait, to prod, to help one of them make the leap.

But when I left the room, our uselessness burned in me. We argued the merits of solutions no one could use, while surrounded by people who we could be helping. To be clear, the other sysadmins didn't see that opportunity for change. They knew they were in pain, but not the cause, or even that there was a fix. Our group was like doctors arguing over theoretical cures while surrounded by the sounds of suffering. I had been having the same argument with the same people for three years, and all that had changed was my tolerance. I was still stupid, they were still right, and no one was any better off.

It was clear that everyone else was content to sit around talking. I was not. I had to move. We were short on action, not ideas. I looked around the room, and I couldn't see who the entrepreneur was. It had to be me. Not because I was right. Just because I was willing to stop talking and get to work. Because I cared more about helping people in the larger community than winning an argument in this elite one.

This freed me to write Puppet, an automation framework that could capture and replicate all the menial work. Through consistency and fast response times, my customers got rid of most of their fires. As we scaled, I had the joy of my users spontaneously thanking me for rescuing their careers, getting them promotions, helping them spend more time with their family and less time on call.

With one foot in the sysadmin camp and the other in the automation subgroup, but really belonging to neither, I was able to move the whole community.

OBSESSION

"The passion which seizes the noble man is a peculiarity, without his knowing that it is so: the use of a rare and singular measuring-rod, almost a frenzy: the feeling of heat in things that feel cold to all other persons: a divining of values for which scales have not yet been invented: a sacrificing on altars which are consecrated to an unknown God: a bravery without the desire for honor: a self-sufficiency which has superabundance: and imparts to men and things."

In other words: A noble man has exceptional passion, but does not realize just how unusual it is: he has high standards for success, enthusiasm for things that others find dull, a sense of what will be valuable in the future, intense but unexplained motivations, courage without the need for praise, and the ability to sustain and revel in this intensity without support from others.

You may have noticed that this chapter is titled *Obsession*, but Nietzsche seems to be talking about passion. For several years, Brad has written and spoken about the pitfalls of "passion" in entrepreneurs, distinguishing it from "obsession," which is a quality he looks for. Dictionaries generally speak of passion as a strong emotion, while obsession is a preoccupation of the mind. We have a hunch that Nietzsche is trying to make a similar distinction here. The word "obsession" did not come into common use until later. Earlier in the text, he says, "What then makes a person 'noble'?...Certainly not that he generally follows his passions; there are contemptible passions." It is worth asking yourself whether you are obsessed with your business and the problem it solves for customers or merely passionate about it.

If you intend to disrupt an industry or change the world, you must expect people to see you as crazy, intransigent, and possibly sociopathic. Maybe you are. To sustain yourself and your efforts in such a climate, you must find your drive within. You must know your vision and why it matters to you. Importantly, you cannot feel that its correctness depends on your ability to explain it to others. You must be obsessed.

Even after you are successful, do not expect universal praise for your vision and persistence. Be prepared for a lawsuit from someone who thought he had the idea first or who thought he contributed to your success. Those whose livelihoods are displaced by the disruption will try to make you look heartless. People will criticize your newfound wealth, even as they use and enjoy your products. The transition from disdain to envy and hostility could be quite sudden.

Consequently, you must pursue your vision and your business for your own purposes. This does not mean that you should ignore sincere advice. It does mean that you should expect no one to fully understand or to have the same level of intensity and intrinsic drive toward the goal you seek. The people who work for you, invest in you, buy from you: most of the enthusiasm they have about your goal will come from you. It can be an immense burden if you do not feel obsessed strongly at the start, if it does not "*seize*" you as "*almost a frenzy.*" Be ready for it.

For more on the importance of obsession, see *Persistence* and *Work as Reward*. For more on potential pitfalls of success, see *Shadow of Success*.

A Narrative from Bre Pettis
CO-FOUNDER AND CEO, MAKERBOT

Shortly after starting MakerBot, I hitched my soul to its destiny. My life at the beginning of 2009 was saturated with goodwill. I was a creative philanthropist: I had spent the previous four years creating content, making value with my own two hands. I amplified that value by freely giving it away on the Internet, for others to build on. I got to know many of the creative Internet pioneers during 2004-08 and I was interested in utopias. I imagined a utopia where endless value could be created from ideas made physical with computer controlled tools.

MakerBot started in January of 2009 with its own utopian business model. Our utopian ideal was that we would design things and share those designs. Users would improve on our designs and share them back; MakerBot would get the benefit of those user-created improvements and make them available for sale to everyone. My friends with business experience told me this was business suicide and that if we ever built a great machine, it would be knocked off. I egotistically laughed at them, and told them that our business model made us so limber that we could out-innovate any competitor.

In my early fundraising pitches I touted MakerBot's openness as a huge advantage for the company. Nietzsche talks about the passion which can seize the noble man. I can verify the intoxicating effect. It was also a brilliant feeling to believe in something that didn't make sense to other people. In 2009, a 3D printer was as confusing to the public as a time machine.

The MakerBot team launched the MakerBot Replicator, and consistent with our model, we published the plans. The knockoffs began. I eventually made an unpopular decision to shift away from our pure utopian business model: with the MakerBot Replicator 2, we would get a design patent on the way it looked, so that knockoffs would at least have to make it look different. My goal to have a company that empowered creativity was stronger than my desire to prove out a risky utopian business model. Unfortunately, the design patent didn't stop the knockoffs, and their customers would even call MakerBot support when they had problems. This drama didn't stop us. In retrospect, even though it tore me up not to have my decision universally accepted, it was clear that it was the right decision for a future filled with creativity-empowering MakerBots.

In 2013 MakerBot changed a lot. The MakerBot Replicator 2 Desktop 3D Printer had fresh branding and sales grew like wildfire. The company was hiring fast and cycled through employees almost as fast. With all the stress of change, some employees stopped performing and others quit in a rage. I have a flaw of wanting people to like me, so I would often wait too long to fire people, which would bring on more resentment when I would finally let them go. Some sued me. Some hated me and the company, but wanted stock in what we had created. In the middle of the year, the company was acquired.

There is a film that came out in the middle of the maelstrom about the 3D printing industry. I had given the filmmakers deep access to our operations and personnel. I expected the movie to document the hard work and success we were having; instead, they focused on the drama of my shift away from a purist utopian business model. They painted that moment as a fall from grace instead of a learning moment. They interviewed ex-employees who were bitter; they focused on the drama of a guy making guns with 3D printers; they painted me as a failure for not living up to my ideals.

I have been Nietzsche's sociopath. I have had to go deep and drive from within against the odds. I have suffered my inability to attain universal praise. I have supported great people and amazing teams who have done the undoable. I have fired good people and I have been seen as heartless. I have been criticized for success while seeing my team's work praised and utilized. I felt the shift from disdain to envy and hostility. I am thankful that I don't suffer from depression, and that I had started to develop internal emotional tools to accept the brutal nature of humanity in parallel with my optimism. I feel a strange sense of honor and simultaneously suffering for having thrived through the whole thing.

The life of passion with all its consequences is a path that incurs deep emotional costs. For those who are called to bring new things into the world, I wish you all the support and friendship in the universe to get you through.

WORK AS REWARD

" But still there are rarer men who would rather perish than work without delight in their labor: the fastidious people, difficult to satisfy, whose object is not served by an abundant profit, unless the work itself be the reward of all rewards. "

In other words: There are rare individuals who would rather die than work without enjoyment: such people are very particular about the quality of the work, and making money is secondary to the reward of the work itself.

Are you obsessed with your business, or are you doing it for the money? Entrepreneurs can be successful with almost any motivation if it is strong enough. Each has its advantages and pitfalls. An obsessive entrepreneur is more inclined to persevere through difficulties, but she may also have difficulty making clear-eyed decisions at times. A financially motivated entrepreneur will emphasize genuine opportunities, but he may lack a core mission to keep the company focused and may be more inclined to throw in the towel. Some of the most motivated entrepreneurs are primarily trying to prove something to their family or friends, or to wreak revenge on their enemies. Some successful entrepreneurs have more interest in doing things well, whatever they are, and the actual product or service is secondary.

Your obsession may not line up with market opportunity. The popular adage "find what you love and do that for a living" suggests that one can make a living doing anything. Depending on what it is, though, it may require that you forego many comforts or consistency in your lifestyle. Only a tiny fraction of artists, poets, and musicians make more than a basic living. The same is true of entrepreneurship: only a small fraction of business ideas prove fruitful, and even fewer are disruptive.

Note carefully how Nietzsche puts it. For this sort of rare individual, making money is not enough, *unless* the work itself is a reward. He is not talking about someone who eschews financial considerations entirely. Smart investors look for entrepreneurs who are obsessed, but they must be obsessed with an idea that will also *make money*. The two things must line up, or it is unlikely to be more than a lifestyle business—if it is successful at all.

Do you understand your own motivations thoroughly? Are you obsessed with the product? Do you want to disrupt the establishment? Do you want to make money so you are free to pursue an intrinsic, non-economic passion? Do you primarily just want to avoid working for someone else? For most people, each of these has its place, but the weighting varies. What is your weighting of these and other factors? Understand your motivations prior to aligning them with the business needs.

For more on obsession as a source of motivation, see *Obsession*. For more on opportunities that match up with investor motivations, see

Domination. For more on the importance of matching your business goals with your motivations, see *Finding Your Way* and *Sustaining Intensity.*

A Narrative from Jud Valeski

FOUNDER & FORMER CEO OF GNIP,
PHOTOGRAPHER, AND ANGEL INVESTOR

After becoming CEO of Gnip (from CTO) I learned of a deal that had recently been signed without my knowledge. I immediately dove in to understand what we'd signed up for. I found the deal to be very lucrative for us; however, it would take our product and engineering team away from our core product vision, and instead, essentially, dedicate us to working on functionality that the other party needed in their product. For all intents and purposes, the deal would contort our idea and turn us into a consulting firm; not what any of us had signed up to do or become.

The deal had already been signed. I had to determine whether or not I was going to go back on our company's word, in order to save our product roadmap, vision, and culture. Breaking the deal would tarnish our deal-making reputation, and increase our financial stress. However, breaking the deal would also allow us to stay true to our desires and vision. I, and the team, were in this for something bigger than just the dollar. I phoned the other party, apologized, explained our need to break the deal, that I understood the implications of doing so, and that we would not proceed with the effort. The other party was of course quite upset, as now their roadmap was in jeopardy, but respected my decision.

The scenario wound up revealing our true motivations, and importantly, how far we were willing to go to honor them.

DELIGHT IN YOURSELF

> " 'Have joy in the endeavor,' people say; but in reality it is joy in oneself by means of that endeavor. "

In other words: They say you should love what you do, but this is really a way of loving yourself through what you do.

When you start a business, you think about changing the world, how you are going to make money, how you will organize and motivate a team, and many other factors large and small. You have a vision for the future and are willing to put forth the blood, sweat, and tears required to see your vision realized. Presumably, you expect to gain satisfaction from seeing that vision realized, whether that satisfaction comes from making the world a better place, from the financial wealth you gain, or some of each.

If you are self-aware, you realize that it is not just the destination that you need to enjoy, but the journey. This is a well-worn adage, apparently even in Nietzsche's time. Yet it is worth emphasizing: most businesses take a long time to reach fruition, and some never do. If what gets you out of bed in the morning is merely the desire for the outcome and not the daily substance of the effort, your enthusiasm and drive will be challenging to sustain. Even if your desire for the outcome is sufficient for you as an individual, your lack of enjoyment of the process may be reflected in the organization's morale. Having delight in the *ongoing* enterprise is important for its ultimate success and realizing your vision.

Reflect on the fact that you started a business—your business. This shows that you are the sort of person who takes initiative and cares about making things happen in the world. That you are the sort of person who enjoys the people, the technology, the thinking, and the leadership elements of starting and building a business. Yes, you delight in aiming to achieve your vision; yes, you delight in the every-day tasks that are involved in that effort; but you also delight in yourself, as being (or becoming) the sort of person who actually does those things instead of simply dreaming or talking about them.

Delight in the process and delight in yourself, whether or not you ultimately realize your vision!

For more on the importance of having both a vision and the drive to make it real, see *Genius*. For more on the importance of maintaining enthusiasm for the effort, see *Patience in Disruption* and *Sustaining Intensity*. For further thoughts on entrepreneurship as personal development, see *Shadow of Success* and *Surpassing*.

A Narrative from Jacqueline Ros
CEO AND CO-FOUNDER, REVOLAR

I love my job. I fall asleep thinking about Revolar. I wake up thinking about Revolar. I dream about Revolar. I love what I do, and I consider myself lucky to have a co-founder who is not only my partner in crime, but equally in love with what we're building. I consider myself blessed to have investors and team members who believe in our mission (use technology to make society better and help communities become safer and healthier). But like any relationship, love is a choice. Like a good "chick flick" (for which I am a notorious sucker) it's easy to fall for the trap that "all you need is love." Love will sustain anything, right? The truth is that it won't.

Someone once told me that in a startup, the team is a direct reflection of the co-founders. In an early employee interview, I repeated this and said that if it were true, I was humbled and honored that such incredible people would work with us and commit to our mission. The interviewee replied that my statement was powerful, and it showed that I had clearly learned to love and be at peace with myself.

This next part is hard to write. I am a first time CEO. Like any first-timer I had certain delusions. You have to be delusionally confident to make it to the next level. I remember time and again thinking that I won't make those mistakes that cost people I deeply care about their jobs. I won't be heartless like I felt so many other CEOs were.

In the last couple months I have been deeply humbled. My empathy for the decisions I've seen other CEOs make has grown by leaps and bounds; I find myself wanting to reach out to them and apologize for the thoughts I had, even though they had no idea I thought them. I've had to look myself in the mirror and ask, "If my team is a direct reflection of me, and now here I stand having made mistakes or hit obstacles beyond my control, which parts of me, which parts of my team, do I choose to cut off for the sake of growth?"

At moments like this, I lean on my co-founder, who in so many ways is my rock. I had hit a real low. A new low I didn't even realize I could hit. She said to me, "Jackie, I know it's hard, but we owe it to all of those who are hustling like crazy and who have invested in us to take care of Revolar, even if that means hurting people we care about." We were discussing an upcoming decision to dismiss several people from our 26 person team, and even writing this hurts.

Love is a choice. I've had to choose to love myself again in order to re-fall in love with the Revolar journey. I've pushed myself personally to places I never thought I'd have to explore. I've learned everyday to re-fall in love with the ups and downs. To re-fall in love with my humanity and how it affects my growing and dedicated team. I've learned to re-fall in love with everything from the most minute details to the larger strategic moments. But most importantly, I learned that every day is a choice and that every day I choose to fall in love with the imperfect journey that is Revolar. I love my job because I love the journey. My new guiding principle: make the choice daily to let the journey make me a better, more realistic, more empathetic person.

MATURITY AS PLAY

“ The maturity of man—that means, to have reacquired
the seriousness that one had as a child at play. ”

*In other words: Real maturity is returning to the focus
and intensity that children have when they play.*

Observe young children immersed in play. Their focus is intense, and
they flow from one idea to the next without pause. Sometimes they
repeat their actions or statements for no apparent reason, other than
the fact that they enjoy performing them. They are neither self-con-
scious nor do they care whether anyone is watching. Sometimes they
create or build something. They are just as likely to gleefully destroy it
as to proudly show it to someone. Other times they just play. They are
serious about it; indeed, much more serious than they are about any
chores they might be assigned.

Compare this to experienced employees, whether managers or individual contributors. There is a seriousness, but it seems different and

feels like it is motivated by external needs and obligations. It often has an edge of impatience or frustration. There might be boredom. The seriousness is *intentional*. They care because they are *paid to care*. One often thinks of this as maturity, or colloquially "adulting": to buck up—to do things one doesn't want to do, because someone needs to do them.

Someone needs to do them—in the service of a larger purpose. Simon Sinek, in his book *Start with Why*, says that the purpose, the "why," transcends the "what" and the "how." If you can connect your daily activities to that larger "why," then you have reached a new level of maturity. You do things because they are part of the playspace in which you are operating, not because someone pays you to do them. The bureaucrat who resists your initiative is just a character in your game. Your engineering team is a plastic motorboat in your bathtub. Their technical difficulties are like your knee poking out of the tub, blocking its route. Victories celebrated by your team are pure joy, like a Little League championship. In this way, you can proceed with focus and seriousness in the moment, driven not by an obligation or a paycheck or even an exit, but by the enthusiasm and sheer joy of the process of achieving the larger purpose. You will see both the obstacles and celebrations as part of the fun.

You need maturity and courage to see the world this way. Our role models for work, and for adult seriousness, are often of the intentional kind. Some people think this intentional seriousness is the proper way to behave. They will see you as frivolous if you seem to be enjoying yourself too much. Ignore these judgments, or persuade those people otherwise.

Once you have mastered this approach to work for yourself, take it further. Figure out how to enable or facilitate your team to see their work as part of the "why," as serious play. It is even more fun and absorbing to play with friends!

For more on Nietzsche's "child" in disruptive entrepreneurship, see the introduction to the *Free Spirits* section. For more on the importance of your creative instincts, see *Deviance*. For more on enjoying the journey, see *Delight in Yourself.*

A Narrative from David Cohen
CO-FOUNDER, TECHSTARS

SPHERO

Thinking about kids immersed in play immediately brings to my mind the story of Ian and Adam, the creators of Sphero.

When they joined the Techstars program, they were working on a garage door opener that you could control with your smartphone. We could tell they were extremely talented, but similar products were already on the market. We challenged them to come up with something more intriguing.

They started brainstorming, and when they came up with an idea for a robotic ball, they lit up – just like little kids. They were excited about the idea, not because they thought it would make money, but from a personal and genuine interest. They didn't understand how it could be a business. They had no idea what it could become or how powerful it would ultimately be. They just thought it would be challenging and fun to create a robotic rolling ball. Which is, when you think about it, a really hard thing to do. How do you tell a ball what is forward or backward or left or right?

Well, they figured out all that engineering, and people loved the product. Even President Obama had fun playing with Sphero. Then Ian and Adam, along with Sphero CEO Paul Berberian, ended up in our Disney Accelerator, where Walt Disney Co. CEO Bob Iger was a mentor. Iger showed them pictures of the BB-8 droid from the upcoming Star Wars movie, The Force Awakens, and asked if they could bring it to life. Disney ultimately licensed the Sphero BB-8 and it became a best-selling toy that holiday season. On the first day the product was available, more than 2,000 sold per hour and the toy was completely sold out by the end of the day.

Sphero now has several products and is a large, successful company. It all began with focusing on a product idea that awakened the founders' inner ten-year-olds.

NEXT BIG SOUND

Simon Sinek's philosophy of connecting to the larger "why" is something we firmly believe in at Techstars. We always want entrepreneurs to do what they love and to start with why, focusing on the bigger reason behind what they're doing.

On their second day in the Techstars program, co-founders Alex, David and Samir informed us that they no longer believed in their startup idea. The concept was for a record label that would use the wisdom of the crowd to promote up-and-coming music artists.

After they decided this wasn't going to be a viable business, they sat in the Techstars conference room and started listing out a bunch of startup ideas. Looking at their list of a dozen ideas, my first observation was that nine of them were related to the music industry. So I said, "Guys, it's clear that you love music. Why are we even talking about these other ideas?"

They responded that the other ideas just made sense, and were solid businesses that would likely be successful. But this sounded like the "intentional seriousness" described above, and is where the "why" comes into play. You can't be driven by passion and joy if you're just pursuing a sensible business idea, and starting a company is too hard if you're working in an area that you don't absolutely love. These guys had nine ideas for music-related startups, so it was obvious that they should build a music startup.

The idea they selected was Next Big Sound, which went on to aggregate social metrics into a formula that provides valuable information and *insights for the music industry. Next Big Sound was ultimately acquired by Pandora in a successful exit.*

Because they were driven by their passion for music, the founders were willing to put in the long hours, hard work and focus necessary to start a business. I remember them mocking up what they wanted their offering to look like, long before they had the functionality, and then watching that functionality come to life over time, exactly as they had imagined it early on. From the outside, it looked a lot like play as they followed their imagination forward. They achieved success by listening to their hearts over their heads and developing a business within the context of what they loved.

Building a startup requires using your head, but more importantly, you have to follow your heart. The best entrepreneurs I know simply pursue what they love, and then they figure out how to make a business out of their passion.

GENIUS

❝What is Genius?—To aspire to a lofty aim
and to will the means to that aim. ❞

*In other words: "Genius" means to establish a challenging
goal and do whatever it takes to accomplish that goal.*

In this chapter, we will begin by engaging briefly in etymology (the history and meaning of a word). Bear with us: the potential payoff is gaining a deeper understanding of the significance of your entrepreneurial striving.

In contemporary usage and in Nietzsche's time, the word *"genius"* primarily refers to someone who has superior abilities, whether intellectual, creative, or interpersonal, or to work products that purportedly reflect such abilities. It usually carries the connotation that these abilities are not explainable and are probably innate. This connotation comes from the original Latin, where it shares a common root with the word "genie," which is a spirit that guides the individual.

In opposition to this sense of the word, some have asserted with pithy phrasing that what people call "genius" is really just hard work (e.g., Thomas Edison's "genius is one percent inspiration and ninety-nine percent perspiration") or persistence (e.g., the late 19th-century proverb "genius is an infinite capacity for taking pains"). Some recent research bears this out, and the phenomenon of epiphany (an "Aha! moment") often follows intense effort and concentration on a problem.

Nietzsche's definition combines and augments these perspectives in a novel way. He adds the notion of a goal, along with the "*will*" or drive to achieve it. He recognizes that one cannot work hard and persist without motivation. From his perspective, the will is the source of that motivation and is therefore primary; hard work and persistence are secondary and implicit. Yet the will itself has no explanation, like the genie of the Latin root. Thus in Nietzsche, there is still an unexplained ability, but it relates to motivation, not skills.

What does any of this have to do with your business? Nietzsche's definition of genius sounds like a pretty good start on a definition of entrepreneurship. One could distill the essence of entrepreneurship down to: establish a challenging goal and do whatever it takes to achieve that goal. To distinguish it from other endeavors, like art and science, we should add that the goal is instrumental—that it has a practical benefit in the world. Entrepreneurial goals involve building and deploying better mousetraps, whether the mousetrap is a physical device, manufacturing process, organizational structure, philanthropic innovation, distribution system, or the virtualization of any of these. Putting all this together, one could describe entrepreneurship as instrumental genius.

This goes to the core of what it means to be an entrepreneur and a free spirit. It applies to your entire team, not just to you. You already

know that you and your team are something special and that by starting and building your business you are doing something unusual
and important. But social and organizational demands for humility
require you to downplay this knowledge. Nietzsche's angle on genius,
and our adaptation of it to entrepreneurship, offers a new way to
think and talk about the significance of your efforts, without the nar-
cissistic overtones or the cliché deflection of "it's just hard work." You
have decided on a goal to improve something in the world, and you
have further decided to do what it takes to achieve that goal. It sounds
simple, and it is not bragging. Yet it is rare, and it is genius.

For additional angles on entrepreneurial genius, see *Doing the
Obvious*, *Persistence*, *Patience in Disruption*, and *Obsession*.

WISDOM FROM EXPERIENCE

" From the Practice of the Wise.—To become
wise we must will to undergo certain
experiences, and accordingly leap into their
jaws. This, it is true, is very dangerous. Many
a 'sage' has been eaten up in the process. "

*In other words: There are certain experiences we
must go through to become wise, so we pursue those
experiences wholeheartedly. This is dangerous, and
many would-be wise men are ruined in the process.*

———————————

Book knowledge is all well and good, but there is no substitute for
actual experience. In business, real situations are far more complicated than any theory could cover, and even case studies must be simplified so that students can understand them. If you want to be a wise
entrepreneur and leader, experiences are essential.

Nietzsche does not simply say "To be wise we must undergo certain experiences." Instead, you must *will* to do so. The implication is that such experiences are intentionally selected. He points out that it is dangerous since the experiences that make you wise risk your reputation, financial stability, or relationships.

To become a wise entrepreneur, you must take the leap and start a company. Statistically, you probably will fail. To ultimately succeed, you will likely have to start more than one company during your career. This is part of the reason experienced investors do not view past entrepreneurial failure as a negative, as long as the failure was due to the right reasons. Failure shows that you have done the necessary work to gain wisdom and that you were *willing* to do so.

Aspiring entrepreneurs often want to get more experience before taking the plunge. That is only helpful if it is the right kind of experience. People tend to focus on domains (e.g., software as a service) or functions (e.g., product management) when they seek more experience. This approach might make you knowledgeable, but the knowledge is too specialized to make you wise.

Instead, aim for the messy, painful, and risky experiences that model entrepreneurship. Propose, fight for, and launch a new product. Fire someone who needs to be fired, even if it is politically difficult. Meet with competitors and practice gathering information without giving away too much. Publicly take the blame for a bad decision. Hire great people without knowing exactly what role they will have. Take on a broken customer relationship and try to fix it. Close a deal that no one thinks you can get. Keep your eyes open for thorny high-risk, high-return business challenges and take them on. Through all of it, observe, reflect, and try to understand what happens.

The same advice applies *after* you have started a company. Choosing to undergo these experiences is not a sacrifice. If you succeed at them, it benefits the company; whether or not you succeed, it increases your wisdom. You have to pick well, but practicing and learning how to pick is also part of becoming wise.

Not everyone is cut out for this. Failure and painful experiences can make you wise, but you can also be *"eaten up"* with their personal and emotional costs. Serial entrepreneurs who do not achieve some success burn out. You will need to be resilient and persistent and take pleasure in the wisdom you gain, whether or not it leads to the outcomes you seek.

For more on one of the "right reasons" for failure, see *Information*. For more on situations that produce such experience, see *Red Hot, Overcoming Obstacles, Resolute Decisions, Monsters*, and *Hitting Bottom*.

A Narrative from Brad Feld

CO-FOUNDER AND PARTNER, FOUNDRY GROUP

In late 1993 my first company, Feld Technologies, was acquired by a small publicly traded company co-chaired by Leonard "Len" Fassler. Len and his partner were building their company, later called AmeriData, through a business consolidation strategy then called a "rollup." Len was an expert: AmeriData acquired more than forty system integration firms and became a multi-billion-dollar business. It was the largest independent system integrator when it was acquired for $500 million by GE Capital in 1996.

Working for Len, I learned a lot about buying and selling companies, but I wanted more. I realized that leading a rollup with him would be the ultimate immersive experience in learning how to do it. So, after the GE Capital acquisition, I co-founded Interliant with Len and two other partners. Coincidentally (see the Nietzsche quote), Interliant was originally called Sage Networks.

1996 was early in the rise of the commercial Internet. As websites proliferated exponentially, many entrepreneurs started small businesses to provide the hardware and software infrastructure to host these websites. Similar to the emergence of the Internet Service Provider (ISP) segment, the web hosting market grew rapidly but without a clear and early dominant company. We had a vision for creating such a company by acquiring and consolidating these web hosting firms.

We quickly raised $42 million and set out acquiring companies. I'd never been a co-chairman of a company before, so I followed Len's lead. I'd never bought a company before. We bought twenty-five in four years. I'd never worked with a private equity firm before—our financial partners owned 80% of the company and regularly beckoned us to their offices for meetings. I'd never taken a company public before—we did an IPO in 1999, which we had to execute twice because we failed the first time.

By 2000, Interliant was a 1,500-employee public company with a nearly $3 billion market cap. We'd hired a CEO from one of the largest ISPs, continued acquiring companies, raised another $37.5 million from strategic investors including Microsoft, Dell, Network Solutions, and BMC, and raised $160 million in the public debt markets. I traveled to look at potential acquisitions, holed up in a conference room at our law firm in midtown Manhattan negotiating or working with investment bankers, and talked to a wide variety of people about what we were doing. The intense pace generated enormous chaos, and I was in the middle of it.

I also made every mistake in the book. When the dotcom bubble popped, we had a business that was losing $5 million per month, with no path to additional capital. Our stock price collapsed, causing morale to plunge. Our highly experienced CEO unexpectedly resigned, and our investment bankers abandoned us. We tried to become profitable by laying people off, restructuring the company, and selling some of the assets we had acquired.

We failed. In 2002, Interliant went bankrupt. The equity in our company, once worth billions, was now worth zero. There were lawsuits.

I had learned a tremendous amount about the mechanics of a rollup. But more importantly, I now knew the exhilaration of upside and the agony of downside, and what those mean in the context of a real business. The experience created the basis for much of my business acumen that I've applied over the past twenty years. Even though we ultimately failed, if I hadn't "leapt into the jaws" of these experiences, I would not have learned deeper lessons.

SERIAL ENTREPRENEURSHIP

"The best thing in a great victory is that it deprives the conqueror of the fear of defeat. 'Why should I not be worsted for once?' he says to himself, 'I am now rich enough to stand it.'"

In other words: The best thing about a big success is no longer fearing failure. One thinks, "I now have the resources and emotional strength to take bigger risks."

There are two types of serial entrepreneurs: those who have had a *"great victory"* and those who have not. The former love what they do, and do it with gusto; otherwise, why would they do it again? They often aim higher because they feel that they have proven themselves and want to take on new challenges. Emotionally, they are comfortable with greater risk because they have a success behind them that cannot be taken away. They also have a financial safety net that minimizes economic and lifestyle risks.

After a few failures, the latter can become increasingly risk-averse and inclined toward lesser ambitions. Their goal may shift from becoming successful to avoiding defeat.

Resisting this attitude requires significant emotional fortitude. If you are a serial entrepreneur who has not yet achieved success, consider taking a break. Join a company that is already in the midst of success. This will renew your enthusiasm through a direct experience of victory. Then you can aim to reproduce that experience in your next venture.

Most startups fail. Investors manage this by investing in multiple companies in parallel. Their strategy is that the gains from a few successes will exceed losses from all of the failures. Entrepreneurs, in contrast, can only build one company at a time.

If you are committed to realizing your entrepreneurial vision, you must be prepared to make more than one attempt before succeeding. Once you have succeeded, ever-larger ambitions and risks become tempting and exciting. Thus, serial entrepreneurship is the rule rather than the exception.

For more on seeking a *"great victory,"* see *Domination, Persistence,* and *Patience in Disruption.* For more on the consolations of defeat, see *Wisdom from Experience, Hitting Bottom,* and *Reflecting Your Light.*

A Narrative from Will Herman

SERIAL ENTREPRENEUR, ANGEL INVESTOR,
AND CO-AUTHOR OF *THE STARTUP PLAYBOOK*

My first job was at a startup—Health Care Computer Systems. I didn't know what a startup was or what the company did when I joined. HCCS was just the only company that responded to one of the 50 resumes I sent out looking for a coding job. I thought nothing of the risk at the time, in fact, I quit college and bagged my degree in mechanical engineering at Lehigh University to join the company. I still can't tell if I made the move out of ignorance or just a fundamental belief that things would just work out. As it turns out, they did and they didn't. HCCS went bankrupt 18 months later, but I learned a lot.

In a move testing my ignorance thesis, I started a new company, DataWare Logic, picking up where HCCS left off. Same industry and pretty much the same product idea. Even though I really had no clue about why the first company failed or what was involved in founding a company, I thought I could do it better. It took me about 18 months to fail again— one of those cash flow lessons that everyone reads about.

Two failures in, I thought the startup thing just wasn't my gig. I wasn't upset about it or fearful, I just thought I should try something else. I joined Digital Equipment Corporation. Then, the world's second largest computer company behind IBM, and became fully ensconced in limited responsibilities, big company culture and a large group of very smart people. After a few years of that, the itch to do something more drove me to join a team of those people leaving DEC and starting Viewlogic Systems. Again, whether it was stupidity or faith, I never felt like leaving DEC was a risky move. It just seemed like the next step for me.

Since then, there have been more new companies—Scopus, Silerity, Innoveda—all successful. Along the way, I never considered the first two failures as anything more than learning experiences. The later successes increased my confidence and led me to be even more comfortable with risk and moving as fast as possible without the potential for consequences slowing me down.

SHADOW OF SUCCESS

❝Success has always been the greatest liar—and the 'work' itself is a success; the great statesman, the conqueror, the discoverer, are disguised in their creations until they are unrecognizable; the 'work' of the artist, of the philosopher, only invents him who has created it, is reputed to have created it; the 'great men,' as they are reverenced, are poor little fictions composed afterwards; in the world of historical values spurious coinage prevails.❞

In other words: We do not understand success: we equate it with the result. The accomplishments of statesmen, generals, and explorers overshadow the person who achieved them. Great works of art or philosophy define how the artist or philosopher is perceived. Our admiration of great men begins with their achievements, which is misleading and ignores who they really are as individuals.

In this book, we casually use the words "success" and "successful" dozens of times. What does it mean to be successful in entrepreneurship, and what does that success do to the people who achieve it?

A great company is like great works of other kinds: scientific, artistic, literary, or political. One often judges the greatness of a work on the *scale* of its impact: the number of people it affects, the extent to which it affects them, or the duration of the effects. For a company, this might mean the number of employees or customers, the market capitalization or revenue, or its profitability or publicly traded status.

In addition to scale, one might also consider *quality* to determine greatness. Included in quality is the question of whether a work's effects are *good*. For a company, this might mean a reputation for customer or employee satisfaction, or changing the world in a desirable way. Sometimes success means achieving an *original* vision, but this is not essential if the outcome is sufficiently good at scale, regardless of changes in direction.

What if all of that is just an illusion? What if the product, the organization, the company you are creating, the money it makes, or the problems it solves are not the correct criteria to determine success? What if success is just about you, who you become, and how you change in the process? What if entrepreneurship is just an elaborate prop within which you can become who you are?

In the context of this standard illusion, everything is inverted. You do not create a great company; rather, the company creates who you are. It does so in the minds of others: they come to equate you with the company. They assume that its traits, strengths, and shortcomings are the same as yours. They figure that the best definition of who you are is simply "the one who built that company." They need someone to admire and use you to fill that role. These attitudes affect how you see yourself. It becomes your identity, the dominant narrative of what your life is and has been. That identity is fed by whatever adulation you receive. Still, is it you they admire, or the role that you have come to play in their minds?

By all means, create a great business, but do not allow its instrumental success and the admiration you receive from others to hijack your humanity. You are much, much more than that.

For more on entrepreneurship as a vehicle instead of a goal, see *Delight in Yourself* and *Milestones*.

A Narrative about Robert Plant
SINGER, COMPOSER, AND CO-FOUNDER, LED ZEPPELIN

While we would have liked to have rock legend Robert Plant contribute his story directly, our own account along with a couple of quotes will have to do. It is too good an example to pass up.

There is little question that musical artists, particularly those who form groups or bands, are also entrepreneurs. Successful music groups create and innovate, disrupt markets, and leverage an organization to make it all work. When Led Zeppelin split up following the death of drummer John Bonham, Plant began a solo career. There was tremendous pressure to perform Zeppelin songs, but he resisted, to the great disappointment of fans. There was and still is a chronic push from fans and from his former bandmates for reunion tours. For the most part, Plant has avoided these as well, and in a recent interview with Esquire *he said:*

Led Zeppelin was an amazing, prolific fun factory for a period of time, but it was three amazing musicians and a singer living in the times. Those times. That's not going to stop me doing what I'm doing now.

Instead of letting himself be defined by the great success of Led Zeppelin, Plant continues to make new music and innovate; in true Nietzschean fashion, he continues to "become who he is" through his work:

> *For me, my time has got to be filled with joy and endeavor and humor and power and absolute self-satisfaction. That's not with Led Zeppelin. That's doing what I'm doing right now, with this band, on this tour.*

This attitude is in obvious contrast to many successful artists who are tempted not only by the money involved in playing old hits but also by the easily attainable adulation. Those artists become defined by their past success, not only in the minds of their fans but also in their own. And the inevitable decline in their abilities and in the audience makes their legacy wistful instead of robust.

REFLECTING YOUR LIGHT

"Seeing our Light Shining.—In the darkest hour of depression, sickness, and guilt, we are still glad to see others taking a light from us and making use of us as of the disk of the moon. By this roundabout route we derive some light from our own illuminating faculty."

In other words: When we are depressed and everything seems bleak, we can take some comfort in the way other people respond to us.

———————————

Brad has written and spoken extensively about depression among entrepreneurs as well as his own experiences with depression. Nietzsche, too, may have suffered from it. Though there is no "solution" to depression, this quote offers a palliative that might ease the pain or emptiness. It may also be helpful even if you are not clinically depressed, but things are going badly, you have recently made a big mistake, or are struggling with anxiety about something.

As an entrepreneur, you are a leader. Your co-founders, your team, and to some extent your customers and investors, all work with you because you play an important and positive role for them. They see you as a *"light"* in their lives. It is completely irrelevant in your present dark hour whether you think this is justified or important. The fact that your light shines is inescapable, and recognizing it is not an act of ego or vanity but simply one of acknowledging reality.

Once you have recognized this reality, you can observe your light's reflection. It is visible even if you are inclined to say "so what?" Observe how your presence changes and animates discussions. Observe how people respond to your requests and questions. Notice the level of motivation in your organization, even in difficult times, and recognize that you selected these people, and they selected you to work with. Watch for the reflection and the effects of your light shining. Don't actively minimize it, just see it, like you see the illumination of the moon. If a sense of detachment accompanies your mental state, use that to help see things as a disinterested observer.

You have now recognized your importance in these people's lives and observed and experienced how you affect them. These are simple facts. You may elect to make judgments about those facts in your depressed state. You might dismiss them as unimportant. Sometimes "Imposter Syndrome" is a component of depression—in that case, you may have the thought that these people are making a mistake or that you are a fraud. This does not change the fact that your own light, reflecting off these people and your role in their lives, has now reflected back onto you. You may not enjoy or appreciate it in your depressed state, but it is there and worth acknowledging. No matter how dark the world may seem, it would be darker without you. It would also be darker if you did not have those other people to reflect your light.

This scenario also suggests action you can take if others around you are down or depressed. Be present with them, and let their light reflect off you. Don't try to generate light of your own by being excessively perky and optimistic. Instead, let the fact of the other person and your enjoyment of them shine, even if their psychological state dims your experience. Be with them and be glad to be with them.

For perspectives on the role of failure in entrepreneurship, see *Information*, *Hitting Bottom*, and *Wisdom from Experience*.

A Narrative from Brad Feld
CO-FOUNDER AND PARTNER, FOUNDRY GROUP

While attending the Consumer Electronics Show in January 2013, I found myself in a dark Las Vegas hotel room, covering my head with a pillow, completely uninterested in dealing with anything. It was the start of a major depressive episode that lasted almost six months.

It appeared that my life was great. Foundry Group was doing well, and my marriage was solid and happy. But as I figured out later, I was physiologically and psychologically exhausted due to an utter lack of self-care, and this triggered the episode. I'd been clinically depressed before and recognized the symptoms. I knew that eventually it would pass, but I didn't know when, or what would bring relief.

My experience of depression is the complete absence of joy. I'm functional and able to do my work, but it takes all of my energy to get out of bed, out of the house, make it through eight hours, and get back home. In the evenings, I don't have interest in anything—food, reading, TV, sex, or exercise. I sit in the bathtub or lie in bed and stare at the ceiling, eventually falling asleep.

My first depressive episode in 1990 lasted two years. I was afraid I would feel that way the rest of my life, and I was incredibly ashamed of being depressed. Dave and I were business partners at the time, and he was one of the few people who knew about it. He didn't really know what to do but was still profoundly helpful.

By 2013, Dave and I had talked about depression enough that he knew exactly what to do this time. He conspired with my assistant to get on my calendar, showed up at my office, and asked me if I wanted to go for a walk. I'd say "Sure" and we'd walk. Sometimes we'd talk. Sometimes we didn't. He spent an hour outside, just being with me. He didn't try to solve my problem, he didn't try to cheer me up, and he didn't try to help me fig- ure anything out. We were just together—two friends who loved and cared about each other.

By being with me, he reflected my light back on me. I eventually figured out what he was doing and felt less depressed when he showed up. The joy hadn't yet returned, but I was glad to be with him.

LEADERSHIP

For deep reasons arising from his ethical project, Nietzsche admired leaders throughout history and observed their behavior. *Leadership* is also an elemental component of entrepreneurship. However, we often conflate leadership and management, and misunderstand the dynamics of leadership.

As companies grow, leaders often get caught up in every aspect of the business. While frequently necessary early on, micromanagement is your enemy and distracts from leading the overall business and organization.

The implementation details of leadership vary, but there are common themes across all approaches. These include messaging, style, decision-making, and appreciation of the work of the team. If you do these poorly, you will undermine or limit your effectiveness as a leader. Nietzsche helps us navigate the opposition between strength and enlightenment in leadership.

Many view extroverted behavior as a fundamental component of leadership. Yet some of the most successful leaders are introverts. Self-promotion and salesmanship are often viewed as positive attributes in leaders. While they can provide an advantage, many extraordinary leaders have mastered the idea of "we" instead of "me," and the concept of servant leadership has recently emerged.

As you consider each quote, reflect on how you initially interpret it. Come back to it after reading the chapter, and reconsider it. Are you growing and evolving as a leader with experience? Are you challenging your own view of your strengths and weaknesses?

TAKING RESPONSIBILITY

> "'I did that,' says my memory. 'I could not have done that,' says my pride, and remains inexorable. Eventually—the memory yields."

In other words: I remember doing it, but that is not who I really am. Eventually, my self-image wins, and I forget that I did it.

Your ego is your greatest ally and your most cunning competitor. To persist through the inevitable difficult times requires deep confidence in yourself and your goals. It is crucial for projecting leadership. You instinctively understand that protecting your pride and confidence is important, which can shape your perception of reality and history.

In this aphorism, Nietzsche highlights the most egregious form of defense: explicitly denying your own actions to yourself or others. You may not go that far, but almost everyone rationalizes: "I could not have done that, *except...*" Instead of denying the action itself, you deny responsibility for it.

But isn't this the same thing? You assert that you didn't *really* do it—you acted in response to misinformation or a lack of information. You rationalize that you were left no choice by circumstances; normally your action would have been fine, but bad luck intervened. You are a victim, not a culprit.

Thinking this way can become a habit, particularly when events are not going the way you want them to. You might notice that it works initially, but it eventually loses its effectiveness among other people. They realize that bad things are happening, but you are somehow never responsible for them. It is always someone else's (or no one's) fault. People come to see you as either someone with generally bad luck or someone who won't take responsibility. Either of these views undermines your effectiveness as a leader.

Is there a way to protect your pride when you make mistakes, without becoming addicted to excuses? Here are some tactics:

Recognize that you make many decisions and take many actions each day, and will therefore make a proportionate number of mistakes. This is not an excuse for any individual mistake, but a recognition that they are normal.

Take responsibility for *all* of your decisions and actions. Recognize the good decisions as well as the bad.

Distinguish between taking responsibility and feeling shame. The former is necessary; the latter, while it may be a signal that you need to change behavior patterns or apologize to someone, is not productive to sustain for long. In another aphorism, Nietzsche suggests that remorse merely adds a second stupidity to the first one.

Distinguish between making the right decision prospectively and retrospectively. The difference between the two consists of information and knowledge, and this gap should drive learning. In particular, you will want to learn more about the issues that, in hindsight, caused your incorrect decision. You will also want to know what sort of information gathering you should have performed in advance of that decision.

Taken together, these tactics can help you move forward with your confidence resting on a more stable foundation. Instead of thinking of each mistake as a threat to your pride, you put that mistake in its proper place and use it to drive learning and improvement. Your pride is justified, not because you are always right, but because you make the best decisions you can, given the state of your knowledge, and constantly work to improve that knowledge. You can take responsibility without feeling the need to rationalize.

For more on treating decisions as a source of learning, see *Information*. For more on handling your confidence in decisions, see *Strong Beliefs* and *Resolute Decisions*. For more on the impact of deception, see *Trust*.

A Narrative from Seth Levine
MANAGING DIRECTOR, FOUNDRY GROUP

Startups frequently miss their sales targets or other key performance indicator goals. Along with most other VCs, I consider this normal and not particularly alarming in and of itself. Most of the CEOs and founders we work with take a critical view of the underlying metrics, surface the key data to their board and investors, and are good about taking responsibility and admitting mistakes. This helps us improve decisions, make adjustments as necessary, invest wisely, and hopefully make the numbers the next time. That said, we occasionally come across executives who have trouble understanding or admitting their role in the decisions that led up to a miss, and instead look to blame external factors or other people.

Many years ago, I worked with a CEO who was unmatched in this tendency. The company was in enterprise software, so the deals were few but large – mid six-figure to even a few seven-figure deals. The market for the company's product wasn't exactly new, but their take on it was an evolution from prior competitors and, in our minds, potentially disruptive in a well-established industry. The original CEO, who was a co-founder of the business, had been a good fit for the early days of the company, but had moved on when it became time to really scale the business. The company's strategy was supposed to involve a transition from highly customized projects for these large customers to a more "productized" offering. This is not an uncommon trajectory for a startup enterprise software business, and the new CEO was brought in specifically because of his background in sales and in productizing software.

Despite the new CEO's experience, the company continually fell short of its sales goals, and there was always an excuse. The development efforts for the transition were consistently behind schedule, and in a vicious cycle, the salespeople were not able to sell it in "product" form. Apparently, none of this was due to decisions made or actions taken (or not taken) by the CEO. Instead, the senior members of the sales team, whom he had hired, were at fault. The market was at fault. The customer's understanding of the product was at fault. The product development team wasn't moving fast enough and was at fault. In the technical arena, the CTO (who was a co-founder of the business) was the problem. The CEO could not look back and say, "I did that" and was, in retrospect, always looking to create conflict between executives to distract from his role in what wasn't working.

Despite the shortfalls and excuses, the company did grow to a few million in annual revenue, even as it continued to lose money and struggled to demonstrate high growth potential. Unable to support the continued excuses of the CEO, the CTO/co-founder eventually quit and started a new (non-competitive) company. Given the issues with the business, a few of the employees left and joined the now ex-CTO in his new venture.

What ensued was an almost unnatural obsession by the CEO to blame all the current and historical difficulties on the departed CTO. For perspective, the business had around forty people at the time, and perhaps three of them left to join the CTO. Every conversation with the CEO eventually turned to the subject of the "damage" the ex-CTO did by leaving and hiring these departed employees. The board of the company was trying to get him to focus on the business and ultimately on selling the company, as access to additional capital was unlikely. But the CEO couldn't focus on anything but the departed CTO, and eventually he even threatened legal action. Board meetings were consumed with his anger at the ex-CTO rather than the prospects for a company sale. Going beyond a passive "memory yielding to pride," this CEO consumed all his energy to demonstrate that he was not responsible for the company's lackluster outcome, even as that outcome hung in the balance.

DOING IS NOT LEADING

"No stream is large and copious of itself, but becomes great by leading and receiving on so many tributary streams...It is only a question of someone indicating the direction to be followed by so many affluents; not whether he was richly or poorly gifted originally."

In other words: A river cannot become large without the streams that flow into it. It provides the direction of the flow, but the water all comes from tributaries. It doesn't matter how big the river was at its source.

––––––––––––––––––––

Sometimes it seems as though it would be easier to run a business all by yourself. You would have no employees to manage, no co-founders or executives disagreeing with you, and no investors applying pressure. Some entrepreneurs actually do this; others do it as long as possible. However, this approach limits how fast your business can grow and eventually how large it can get. It can also be difficult for you to sustain your motivation and energy when operating alone.

Once you decide to grow your business beyond yourself, you have committed to building it through an organization. This marks a significant shift in your personal contribution and priorities. No longer are the details of product development, sales, customer service, and finance your direct concern. Instead, you now need to focus on building an organization that can perform these activities with excellence and consistency. While there is a transitional period where you remain involved in operational issues, you increasingly spend your time and energy on people, culture, processes, and the overall direction of the business.

This idea is often difficult to accept or understand. Once you grow your business beyond yourself, your job is not to grow and run the business. Your job is to build and lead an organization that will grow and run the business. It is a different job that requires different skills and emphasis.

The benefits of this shift are transformative. The strength of your business now has no connection to your personal bandwidth or your own abilities in particular areas. Executives and managers, though led by you, now drive the growth of your business. Think of it as a great river whose headwaters initially grow through small tributary streams but which later grows faster by merging with other rivers.

Growing a business is not as simple as water flowing down a hill. You must pick and choose which tributaries to accept into the flow. You must pick the right path so as not to drain into a stagnant pond. You must work to avoid having the stream split into different directions. Building and leading an organization is challenging and arduous. It is your job. How well you do it will determine the success of the business.

For more on the transition from contributor to leader, see *Introverts, Faith, Attracting Followers,* and *Two Types of Leaders.*

A Narrative from Matt Blumberg

CEO, BOLSTER, AND AUTHOR OF STARTUP CEO AND STARTUP CXO

I recall one particularly painful month when I better understood the need to focus on making the organization work. We finally had a full management team and a real Board in place, but I did everything backward. I created a whole set of materials for an all-hands meeting, then held a Board meeting that required a new set of materials that were even more detailed, then had to host a second all-hands meeting to cover some of those additional details, then I had my quarterly management offsite where we made some decisions that changed direction, forcing me to go back both to the Board and to the whole team with yet another set of materials and talking points.

After a few situations of that kind, I realized that to get leverage for myself without creating chaos I would need to align purpose and focus across the organization. What evolved was a structure I call our company Operating System. In computing, the operating system is the consistent baseline code that connects the hardware to the software and allows the device to function. Our notion was that a company Operating System would play the same role – connecting the hardware (our people) to the software (their work) and allowing the organization to function.

Our Operating System is just a regular set of behaviors and rhythms that team members can depend on as they make their daily leap into the unknown, including:

- *An advance schedule of major meetings.*
- *A consistent format for major communications.*

- *Clarity around membership in leadership groups and their decision-making.*
- *A rigorously enforced open-door policy.*
- *A single set of IT systems and operational procedures.*

I have found that when we keep these pieces of the Operating System in good working order, our team can be alert and ready to deal with the challenges that really matter.

FAITH

> "One man had great works, but his comrade had great faith in these works. They were inseparable, but obviously the former was entirely dependent upon the latter."

In other words: One man created great things, but his partner had faith in the things that were created. They were a team, but the creator was completely dependent on his partner who had faith.

In the earliest stages of your company, you focus on the product and the market. You and your small team iterate on versions of the product and on potential target markets to find product/market fit. Hopefully, customers start to buy your products in increasing volumes, you begin building an organization, and your leadership transition begins.

The growing business now needs a leader who has an abiding faith in the company's products and shouts it from the rooftops. Along with Nietzsche, we use the word *"faith,"* which largely means "confidence," perhaps with a slightly religious or zealous tone. Whatever your individual role has been in building products and identifying markets, you must now focus on building enthusiasm. Your faith in the products may be the single most important criterion that prospective investors, employees, and partners use to assess the business. If you do not outwardly express great confidence, who will? Only a leader with faith can raise capital and hire a great team.

For an unsurpassed example of what such faith looks like, we recommend that you watch Steve Jobs's introduction of the iPhone from 2007.

Your sales organization is an extension of the enthusiasm-building role, so your attitude about the products is particularly crucial to them. There is a derogatory stereotype that salespeople will sell anything, no matter how bad the quality or irrelevant to the customer's actual needs. This is not accurate; what it reflects is that they have faith, and their faith begins with the head of sales and with the company's CEO. Good salespeople work to develop relationships and build their reputations. Such efforts are investments that make selling easier. If they learn that they are selling products that diminish their reputation and relationships, they will leave the company. Consequently, they must have faith in their company's product quality. Further, salespeople in an early-stage company see themselves as investing in future opportunities to earn more money. They need to have faith that the products are the right thing at the right time for the market, or it will not be worth their while to build that market.

In a technology company, markets shift and technology advances, so its products are being redesigned every day. It is not enough to have faith in current products; a leader must have faith that the team itself can continually produce great works. A startup team works hard, and sustaining motivation is a big factor in long-term success. Philosopher and psychologist William James addresses this beautifully in his essay *The Will to Believe*:

> *A social organism of any sort whatever, large or small, is what it is because each member proceeds to his own duty with a trust that the other members will simultaneously do theirs. Wherever a desired result is achieved by the co-operation of many independent persons, its existence as a fact is a pure consequence of the precursive faith in one another of those immediately concerned. A government, an army, a commercial system, a ship, a college, an athletic team, all exist on this condition, without which not only is nothing achieved, but nothing is even attempted.*

According to this, all the team members must have faith in each other. But this is unsustainable if it does not begin with a leader exhibiting great faith in the product and the team.

As a leader, you cannot simply decide to have confidence in people or their work product. They must earn that confidence. But you do not limit your confidence to what you have seen so far—you take an additional leap of faith. Once you see that the team has the potential to produce, you do not insist on justification in each case, and you simply believe that they will continue to do their work well. Similarly, you cannot afford to have blind confidence that your vision for the company is correct merely because you have fallen in love with the idea. You must make sure that you understand the customers and the market and how the product fits that market before reaching your conclusion. Nevertheless, the conclusion cannot be fully scientific—your belief is ahead of the evidence. You add a little something to your confidence to have faith, yet with a rational foundation.

Don't get your role as a leader backward. Once the business starts to grow, your role is not to be the one who has great works. You are the one who has great faith in the works of your team. You have faith in their works because you believe in the products they have built so far and in their abilities and commitment to continue to build great products. You also believe in the goals you set and the direction you lead. You need your team because they will create these works. But they need you even more, because if no one has faith that their efforts are worthwhile, then those efforts are unlikely to succeed.

For a more general look at the transition from building a business to building an organization, see *Doing Is Not Leading*. For more on the ways a leader can demonstrate faith in the team, see *Gratitude and Integrity*.

ATTRACTING FOLLOWERS

"Men press forward to the light not in order to see better but to shine better.—The person before whom we shine we gladly allow to be called a light."

In other words: People are drawn to light because it shines on them, not because it shows them the way. A person who makes us shine is someone we gladly call a light.

Leaders are people who lead the way. They know their direction and take the first steps. However, this is not the only aspect of leadership. To be a leader, you must also have followers. It is a mistake to think that merely knowing the way and pursuing it will attract those followers. Instead, personal magnetism and charisma are what initially attracts followers.

According to Olivia Fox Cabane in *The Charisma Myth: How Anyone Can Master the Art and Science of Personal Magnetism*, charisma is not an inborn feature of your personality but a tool that you develop and use. It does not require you to be an extrovert. Cabane breaks charismatic behavior into three core components: presence, power, and warmth. Combined in the right way, through both words and body language (and mediated by your mental state), these three behaviors will draw people to you.

Presence and warmth are not about you, but about how you act toward others. Presence means that you are genuinely engaged in your interactions with a person and are listening and attentive. Warmth means that you show concern for and interest in them and their well-being. It suggests to them that you might be inclined to use whatever power you have to help them. These behaviors are similar to shining a light on someone. Cognitive psychologists often compare attention to a spotlight, and light is also associated with heat.

In *How to Win Friends and Influence People*, the eighty-year-old perennial bestseller, Dale Carnegie makes these same points, though presenting them differently. He suggests becoming genuinely interested in other people, being a good listener, talking in terms of the other person's interest, and making the other person feel important in a sincere way. In other words, let them shine.

If you wish to lead, but presence and warmth are not your natural inclinations, you have work to do. Self-improvement is part of your job. You may wish to read Carnegie and Cabane's books. It is important to develop presence and warmth in a genuine way, though the effort will feel artificial at first. Your followers are the people who will build your company. You want them to help you, but can you blame them for wanting to know what's in it for them? Isn't it reasonable that they want you to help them while they are helping you? This is what presence and warmth accomplish: you show your followers that you see a mutual, rather than a one-sided, benefit.

Cabane's third element, power, comes from a number of sources. In leadership, it often relates to the credibility and confidence you have in your chosen direction. People are willing to consider following you because the fact that you know the way gives you the power to help them. A light without power is dark and neither shines on anyone nor shows the way. If you are naturally warm and attentive, you already know about shining the light on others, so focus instead on the perception of your power to help.

In addition to assessing and developing your own ability to attract followers, as your company grows, you will hire leaders in various executive roles. Part of your evaluation process should look at charismatic factors in candidates. This may be difficult in a direct interview because most people are attentive and warm to someone who might hire them. Instead, observing their behavior with others, such as at a group interview lunch, is more effective for this purpose.

As an entrepreneur, you are obsessed with your vision and your desire to disrupt an industry. To succeed, you need others to enthusiastically follow you in that effort. This includes not only employees but also investors and early customers. It is tempting to think that those others will follow you simply because the direction you are showing them is so compelling. That is not enough—they are drawn to you *"not in order to see better but to shine better."*

For more on leading as an introvert, see *Introverts*. For more on self-improvement as part of your job, see *Surpassing*. For detail on why you need your followers to build the company, see *Doing Is Not Leading*. For ideas on appropriately showing power, see *Resolute Decisions*, *Strong Beliefs*, and *Taking Responsibility*.

RESOLUTE DECISIONS

> "A sign of strong character, when once the
> resolution has been taken, is to shut the
> ear even to the best counter-arguments.
> Occasionally, therefore, a will to stupidity."

*In other words: Once a decision is made, a strong leader will shut
down debate. This sometimes seems like stubbornness and stupidity.*

———————

One of the pleasures of leadership is the fact that there are no hard-and-fast rules to follow in all circumstances. Every point has its counterpoint. In the Techstars accelerator, the advice of mentors is a central benefit of the program, but different mentors often provide contradictory advice. Techstars calls this "mentor whiplash." This Nietzsche quote offers such a counterpoint to more familiar advice that encourages learning, information collection, and listening to your team.

You make decisions with imperfect information, and all choices have consequences. Nevertheless, to make any forward progress at all, you must choose a direction. Leaving all your options open for too long means that you aren't pursuing any of them well. Uncertainty and vacillation sap team motivation.

Before you make a decision, you want to hear all the best arguments for and against particular choices. Once you have made the decision, continuing to debate it is detrimental. In the words of Mal from *Firefly*, "Why're you still arguing what's been decided?" There are always naysayers. You must resist them and move on.

Your team will see steadfastness as a sign of strong character and confidence when you take this approach. Those who continue to question the decision will struggle to understand. They wonder why you are not listening. They may see you as simply stubborn, or they may view it as an intellectual failure, "*a will to stupidity.*"

To navigate these contrary forces, remain conscious of what you are doing. During the period when the correctness of the decision remains unclear, you will want to stay the course. When it becomes clear that a decision was wrong, it is time to reconsider. How much mental effort you expend on this depends on the relative importance of the decision, as spending your time revisiting minor past decisions will deplete your energy to make new ones.

Prepare yourself mentally for the post-decision period. Prior to the decision, be aware of things that are likely to go wrong, and decide in advance whether you will continue with your chosen approach if they do. This allows you to reconsider only if you learn new and truly surprising information, while also robbing the naysayers of ammunition.

Most leaders err on one side or the other. If you tend to stick with bad decisions too long, push yourself to listen a little sooner. If you tend to question your decisions, wait a little longer before you entertain dissent. Over time, you want your reputation with your team to reflect that you are steadfast but not stubborn, that you don't change direction at the first sign of difficulty but that you do not wait until it is too late.

Although each decision has a substantive importance of its own, you must weigh the impact of changing direction—or of not considering a change—on your long-term reputation.

For typical counterpoints, see *Leading Gently* and *Groupthink*. For more on communicating decisions, see *Right Messages*. For more on persisting with an idea, see *Persistence*.

A Narrative from David Mandell

CO-FOUNDER AND CEO, PIVOTDESK

We created PivotDesk with the goal of solving a specific pain point that I had endured repeatedly over the course of my entrepreneurial career. Real estate is static and businesses are dynamic. Business owners are constantly forced to bet on how large the business will be over the course of a five or ten year lease. That kind of prediction is rarely accurate even one year out.

Businesses needed a solution that would add flexibility to lease agreements yet fit within the existing real estate infrastructure. Such a solution would enable long-term leaseholders to offset the cost of their lease, while enabling smaller businesses to find space without committing to a long-term lease. PivotDesk accomplished this by creating a sharing marketplace between leaseholders and smaller businesses.

It was my strong belief that the ultimate distributors of the value on the platform would be commercial real estate brokers. This wasn't obvious and, at least at first, some investors as well as some on the founding team were unsure whether it was the correct distribution strategy. The initial feedback from brokers and industry insiders was incredibly negative. In their view, the model we were pushing would never be adopted by the existing players. They thought we would end up as just another silly idea that tried to capitalize on the commercial real estate industry.

I was convinced that this was the only way to truly grow the marketplace at scale, and worked to lay out a long-term strategy. This strategy eventually led to broker distribution, but relied initially on targeting the business owners directly. They were the ones suffering the pain that we were addressing, so it had intuitive appeal. The marketplace grew. Nevertheless, we were continually ignored by industry insiders and were told that brokers would never use us.

Once we had enough momentum from leaseholders, we followed our strategy and pushed hard to launch a broker software platform for PivotDesk. It was designed specifically to enable brokers to take advantage of our marketplace to benefit their customers. We launched, and they didn't use it. They didn't use it at all.

We started hearing alarms in the back of our minds, recalling the predictions that this approach was a waste of time. I pulled the head of product aside and we had a few heart to hearts about the fact that the brokers weren't engaging. Motivating the team became more difficult, and regrouping to try to build the right solution proved daunting.

I was still convinced that this was the correct strategy, but we needed to understand how the brokers worked in much more detail. The team went much deeper on customer exploration by spending time with them. Eventually we made some progress with a few key brokers. We were able to get some positive feedback as they began to understand how they could make more money while helping their customers find better solutions. At that point, things finally started to change. Through continued persistence and with the input of these early adopters, we redesigned the platform in a way that truly fit how they did their daily business. Usage started taking off, leading to partnership agreements with several large commercial brokerage firms.

RIGHT MESSAGES

> "The Disappointed One Speaks.—'I listened
> for the echo and I heard only praise.'"

*In other words: It is disappointing when you are
merely admired instead of understood.*

Coordinated action is a primary goal of leadership. If everyone on your team is working in a different direction, it results in organizational Brownian motion—heat without progress. In this quote, someone Nietzsche calls *"The Disappointed One"* is disappointed because he has not achieved coordinated action. People in the organization have not bought into executing on the vision offered by the leadership. Instead, they talk about how wonderful the vision is, what great and charismatic leaders they have, and other sorts of praise.

As an enlightened leader, you may be bothered by the word *"echo."* You want people to think for themselves rather than echo what you say.

Let us examine this a bit more carefully. An echo is not an exact replica. It sounds *like* the original, carrying the primary signal, but it is modified in various ways. View an echo as team members expressing and acting on the company's direction and vision in their own words.

The quote does not require that the original sound comes from you. Echos may come from anywhere, and it can be difficult to tell where the original sound arose. Whether it is your own vision or one that you developed collaboratively with the team, you want it to resound across the organization. Otherwise, you will lack coordinated action.

The quote isn't distinguishing between people who think for themselves and people who blindly follow. Instead, it is distinguishing the echo—people following the organization's direction—from praise of you, or of the vision, or of the company. Your goal is coordinated action, not admiration.

You should not blame the team for this. It is a failure of leadership and communication. It suggests that you are delivering the wrong message. Perhaps you have a tendency to turn the direction of conversation or speeches toward yourself. In that case, people are echoing what they heard, which is how wonderful you are, and not what you thought you were trying to convey. As one indicator, think about how often you use the word "I" during company meetings.

Another possibility is that you are delivering the right message but in the wrong way. If you present organizational goals from a purely intellectual angle, you will evoke no enthusiasm. People think, "those are smart goals." Conversely, if you offer the goals through a purely emotional appeal, then the team, while enthusiastic, may not really understand the direction or why it is the right one. They say, "this new direction is exciting!" Both cases result in praise without effective action.

If you are the Disappointed One, your message should be the focus of your disappointment. Examine the way you communicate the vision and direction of the organization. Make sure it includes *both* emotional and intellectual components, and that it isn't really about you.

For more on alignment and agreement, see *Groupthink*, *Integrators*, and *Independence of Mind*. For more on the role of emotion in communication, see *Once More with Feeling*.

LEADING GENTLY

“With a very loud voice a person is almost
incapable of reflecting on subtle matters.”

*In other words: When you are talking, you
are probably not thinking too hard.*

A leader must both lead and choose the direction in which to lead. There is a delicate balance between these two roles. Strong leadership communicates a clear direction along with confidence that it is the right direction. This does not leave much room for public deliberation because it risks undermining the confidence of the leader. Team members wonder why you are discussing what you have already decided. Thus the requirements of leading can easily overwhelm the need to choose well.

Your need to project confidence and authority can reduce your own awareness of the subtleties of a situation. You believe in your own position without thinking critically about it. You fail to notice new facts or examine nagging concerns that turn out to be important. Leadership can be a loud voice.

Your voice carries a great deal of weight with the team you lead. This is true whether it is projected at high volume, expressed with powerful confidence, or spoken normally but backed by the authority of your position. You lose the opportunity for feedback if others think that you have made up your mind or that they might be humiliated by disagreeing.

You must find the right balance. Lead, but make sure the loud voice of your leadership does not hinder your ability to gather information and make the right decisions.

For more on feedback after a decision is made, see *Resolute Decisions*. For more on agreement in your organization, see *Groupthink* and *Independence of Mind*. For ideas on how to spend more time thinking about your direction, see *Stepping Back*.

A Narrative from Brad Feld
CO-FOUNDER AND PARTNER, FOUNDRY GROUP

While I was co-chairman of Interliant, we bought about twenty-five companies. Shortly after one of those acquisitions, I visited their offices and was walking down the hall with the founder, having a casual conversation. He mentioned that until now he had only owned used cars, but now, finally, he might buy a new one. I commented on how dingy the wall in the hallway was. I mentally noted his frugality and the scrappy approach of his company.

Returning the next morning, I saw that there was a worker painting that same hallway. When I asked the founder about it, he replied that I had told him the wall needed to be painted. I realized I had left the most important part unsaid—that the dingy wall was good. My "loud voice" as the buyer of his company was both misinterpreted and over-interpreted. After realizing the discrepancy, we had a good laugh about it. And going forward, I worked harder to be clear with people about the point I was making with my comments.

This founder was a strong leader, yet he was prompted to take action that opposed his instincts without giving me any pushback. Imagine the effect of such words—even if they are understood correctly—on a broader team. I always try to keep in mind that because I am a leader, my words influence behavior more than I usually intend, and I do what I can to counteract that.

GRATITUDE AND INTEGRITY

"A man of genius is unbearable, unless he possess
at least two things besides: gratitude and purity."

*In other words: Nobody likes a person who
is smart but isn't honest and nice.*

You may be a person of genius. Perhaps you have the ability to foresee trends in consumer behavior. Perhaps you have a strong vision and will. Or you may employ a genius, such as a head technologist who has an uncanny ability to architect and build efficient software systems.

People who have genius of some sort can be difficult to work with. They are often impatient when others don't understand things quickly. They are sometimes arrogant. They are frequently quirky or socially awkward. They might be extremely demanding, or they may have difficulty focusing and following through. It is easy to see how such a person could be unbearable.

Nietzsche suggests that gratitude and purity are two attributes a person of genius must exhibit in order to avoid this fate. There may be others, but these are the minimum. If you are the person of genius and wish to lead an organization, you will need to develop these attributes. When hiring others, look for these characteristics by making them part of your interview or decision process, even for co-founders. While it is possible that you could help someone develop these attributes, it is unlikely. People only change if they want to, and many geniuses believe they have already figured out the right way to be.

Gratitude has two flavors in the context of genius and entrepreneurship. The first is gratitude for your own abilities. In some cases, the term has an object: you are grateful to parents, to teachers, to siblings and friends, or to the giants on whose shoulders you stand. In other cases, you are simply grateful for the genius with which you are endowed. Such gratitude incorporates humility: you are fortunate to have this genius, and you know that it is not something that you developed entirely on your own.

The second flavor of gratitude is toward the other people you work with. Gratitude makes them feel appreciated, and they realize you value the roles that they play. Few things are more unbearable at work than feeling like one's work is not valued. This form of gratitude also expresses vulnerability.

One might interpret purity as integrity—a consistency among beliefs, statements, and actions. A lack of integrity adds up to deceit. When a brilliant person is deceitful, whether intentionally or not, the result is particularly bad. One cannot trust such a person, and the genius may be used in the service of undisclosed or detrimental ends. Purity also means having a sense of fairness. A genius must pull her own weight and should not apply the same expectations to those who are not as fortunate in their natural abilities.

LEADERSHIP · 183

In addition to gratitude and purity, there may be other attributes you want to require of yourself or of any other brilliant person you bring into your organization. These help to constitute your company culture, making it possible for their genius to bear fruit without stifling the work of everyone else. You should endeavor to understand what those other attributes are.

For more on the notion of entrepreneurship as genius, see *Genius*. For more on gratitude as an expression of vulnerability, see *Gratitude*. For more on learning to show warmth, see *Attracting Followers*. For more on the impact of deceit, see *Trust*.

A Narrative from Dave Jilk
FOUNDER AND CEO, STANDING CLOUD

I wouldn't say I'm a genius, but keeping up intellectually has never been one of my challenges. In contrast, I have always found leadership difficult. There are many reasons, but the issue outlined here is probably one of them.

At Standing Cloud, I was consistently frustrated with the level of effort of the technical team. Though they worked diligently while at the office, it seemed that they all had other priorities that caused frequent late arrivals, long lunch breaks, or early departures. There were dogs to feed, workouts to squeeze in, and children's events to attend. Some employees did not even seem to consistently put in forty hours a week. My early experience in startups was that long hours are expected.

Wanting the team to work more was not a pointless control need of mine. We were held back by the pace at which we could introduce new features and try new approaches. If we could have developed capabilities faster, we might have been able to explore product/market fit more broadly. Instead, we were only able to pursue a single technical approach and could only vary the target market.

Initially I tried to set an example by being at the office about sixty hours a week, but that began to seem rather pointless when only the leadership team was there to see it. I tried implementing some of the ideas in Simon Sinek's Start with Why. This didn't make any difference either. I tried a few other tactics. What I did not do is think about it from the team's point of view.

I did have an intuitive sense that negativity was unhelpful, so I tried not to show my frustration. I tried to express appreciation when I found opportunities to do so. All this was forced: I could not feel gratitude because it was blocked by frustration, and this was in turn generated by my expectations. In hindsight, I know that everyone could sense that they were not really appreciated, despite otherwise being treated well. My infrequent expressions of appreciation probably seemed disingenuous. The team undoubtedly sensed that my real goal was to get them to work more and harder.

At some point, I realized that I didn't really want to work that hard either. I had difficulty admitting this to myself, and definitely didn't want to come out and say it to the team, but I was burned out. While I was generally very open and honest with them, I came up short on integrity with respect to this issue. I lacked the purity that Nietzsche speaks of, and in exactly the same subject area as my lack of gratitude.

With these two shortcomings, I was surely unbearable. An unbearable leader is not one you work hard for.

I do not know whether genuine gratitude and purity would have been sufficient to change the outcome for the company. Had I just "relaxed" and become comfortable with the effort the team was putting in, we all might have been happier, but our development pace probably would not have changed. Wouldn't that be doing our investors a disservice? Shouldn't we be giving it our all? I have always thought that working smart and working hard are both necessary to make a startup a success. That to achieve great things one needs high, not low, expectations. If I were to attempt a leadership role again, reconciling these perspectives would be paramount.

TWO TYPES OF LEADERS

❝I praise leaders and forerunners: that is to say, those who always leave themselves behind, and do not care in the least whether anyone is following them or not. 'Wherever I halt I find myself alone: why should I halt! The desert is still so wide!' Such is the sentiment of the true leader.❞

In other words: I praise those who are always looking one step ahead and do not care whether anyone else agrees or follows them. "There is so much to do and see, why should I stop to wait for everyone else?" This is how true leaders think.

In most of the chapters of this book, we present a quote that, as we have applied it to entrepreneurship, we mostly agree with. As we discussed in the Introduction, that does not mean you should agree with us—rather, the presentation is intended as food for thought. The above quote is a little different. For us, it raises difficult questions relating to both leadership and strategy as a business matures. It makes a clear statement about leadership that might be right in some cases and wrong in others. It therefore offers a way to think about your own role and tendencies, and how they fit the needs of the business.

The genesis of a startup is outward-looking: you see an industry, a paradigm, or a way of doing things that you seek to disrupt. This impetus toward disruption is a characteristic of visionary leaders. Such people see the world in terms of what they would like to change and have a tendency toward taking action in that direction. They "*do not care in the least whether anyone is following them or not.*" Sometimes this tendency makes the entrepreneur seem a little crazy. Sometimes it can make the company lose its focus by attempting to disrupt too many things at once. Nevertheless, in the early days of a startup, leadership requires an evolving vision with leaders who, in Nietzsche's words, "*always leave themselves behind.*"

As a business finds product/market fit and works toward accelerating growth and improving margins, leadership requires a different quality. The firm has identified a distinct path that offers continued growth and lucrative results, and it is now accomplishing the intended disruption. Leadership needs to shift its focus to aligning the organization to succeed on that particular path. It must resist the temptation to open additional fronts of activity. Great leaders at this stage are organizational rather than visionary. They may have a vision for strategy and scale but are focused on executing rather than seeking new opportunities. From their perspective, the question of what to disrupt already found its answer.

Some entrepreneurs can navigate this transition from visionary leadership to organizational leadership, but many cannot. It depends on how tightly the notion of continuous disruption is baked into their souls. For some, who always see "*the desert is still so wide,*" the instinct to disrupt anew does not go away just because the business is already in the process of successfully disrupting an industry.

Those who cannot make the transition must either find a new role in the organization, bring on effective organizational leadership, or depart. Some take on a board chair or untethered CTO role, where they can offer an evolving vision of the future to both the industry and the company. Some stay as CEO but bring on a senior leader, in a president or COO role, who has strong organizational skills. Others leave the company and go after disrupting an entirely new industry; or, after non-competition agreements expire, they create a new and disruptively competitive business in the same industry. Founder transition issues can even be a consideration in deciding to sell a company.

We could leave it at that: a question of leadership style at different stages and the attendant entrepreneur transition. But in this era of rapidly accelerating technology change, industry disruption happens almost continuously. Before long, organizational-style leaders whose scaling process is not yet complete find that they are now the target of disruption. They are focused on growing the products that are the original source of the company's success and do not see shifts coming. Dealing with the snake eating its own tail now becomes a strategic issue that needs to be addressed often during a company's growth curve and creates ongoing tension between the need for visionary versus organizational leadership.

Industries have always changed continuously at the level of products and product capabilities. Successful firms must innovate at this level in the everyday course of business. Pursuing this sort of change is merely one component of organizational leadership. Disruption does not arise from building features or enhancing a product line; it operates at the level of substitution effects or ways of life. Uber and Lyft disrupted transportation not because they simply tweaked the taxicab model, but because they created an entirely new way to bring transportation and riders together. Apple disrupted computing because it gave people a way to have their computing and communication devices with them and available at all times. Initially, Uber looked like just another app, and the iPhone looked like a phone with some extra features but lacking a keyboard. When first released, they looked like new products, not disruptions.

When an incumbent firm's leaders have their heads down on the core business, they are unlikely to see shifts like this coming. They need someone in the organization who is not as focused on the core business to bring potentially relevant shifts to their attention. This will help them look away from the trees occasionally to see the forest. This does not mean they will, or should, react to every suspected shift immediately. Instead, it means they are aware of possible directions the industry might head. As a disruptive shift begins to manifest, the organizational leadership will be more prepared and can begin to incorporate the shift into their strategy and development activities.

Rapidly growing startups need visionary leaders as members of the team, even if they are not leading the organization as a whole. Who better to take on this role than the original visionaries who were unable to make the transition to organizational leadership? This requires a certain understanding between the organizational and visionary leaders. The former must have patience with the occasional chaos generated by the latter. The latter must accept that not every idea they advance will be pursued immediately and must avoid trying to influence the mainstream organization. Building the right kind of relationships between these two types of leadership is crucial for long-term success. Losing focus will dissipate the firm's rapid growth, but lack of awareness of industry shifts can short-circuit its opportunity at scale.

Substitution changes and way-of-life changes tend to be moves where you bet the company. Nietzsche's idea of a leader is like someone who regularly bets the company. A firm cannot do this every time the wind shifts, or it will never achieve its potential. But in an era of accelerating change, it cannot ignore the ongoing shifts either. Two kinds of leaders are needed.

For more on the transition to organizational leadership, see *Doing Is Not Leading*. For more on the characteristics of visionary leaders, see *Deviance*, *Obsession*, and *Genius*. For more on the risks of disrupting too many things at once, see *Finding Your Way*. For a look at the difference between alignment and agreement, see *Groupthink*.

INTROVERTS

" My stillest hour spoke to me in a whisper: '...To execute great things is difficult: but the more difficult task is to command great things. This is your most unpardonable obstinacy: you have the power, and you will not rule.' And I answered 'I lack the lion's voice for all commanding.' Again there was spoken to me in a whisper: 'It is the stillest words which bring the storm. Thoughts that come with doves' footsteps guide the world...' "

In other words: I heard a voice that said "Doing great things is difficult, but leading people to great things is even more difficult." I thought to myself, "But I am not a natural leader." The voice continued, "The most dramatic changes come from a leader with a soft touch."

Here Nietzsche addresses one of the more common reasons why you might resist building an organization: you do not see yourself as a leader. A common but misleading conception is that leaders are egotistical extroverts who issue orders in a booming voice. But you are not leading soldiers on a battlefield of bloody hand-to-hand combat. Commanding, in the business world, is much more the art of subtle persuasion. Genuine authority comes from being respected and from the team's desire to please, not from your holding an official position or being the biggest and loudest voice in the room.

If you are an introvert, the challenge seems that much more daunting. You will need to speak in front of large groups at times. At meetings, people will give much weight to both the tone and substance of your comments. Everyone will know who you are; you cannot avert your eyes and keep to yourself. These encounters use up your energy. But you do not need to pretend you are an extrovert. You can interact and deliver messages on *"doves' footsteps,"* in a way that suits your introversion.

Some of the greatest leaders and entrepreneurs in history have been introverts. Bill Gates, Larry Page, and Mark Zuckerberg are all introverted. Abraham Lincoln was an introvert. Mahatma Gandhi, who was also an introvert, said, "In a gentle way, you can shake the world," which sounds remarkably similar to Nietzsche's point. Some recent books are resources for introverted entrepreneurs, including Susan Cain's *Quiet: The Power of Introverts in a World That Can't Stop Talking* and Laurie Helgoe's *Introvert Power: Why Your Inner Life Is Your Hidden Strength*.

This does not mean that anyone can lead. Steve Wozniak, the co-founder of Apple Computer, said, "Work alone. Not on a committee. Not on a team." If you have this inclination, you may need to find a partner who can build a team and lead it while you focus on building products.

To decide whether a leadership role is right for you, work to understand yourself along with what leadership truly requires. You do not need a *"lion's voice for all commanding."* You do not need to be extroverted or loud. You do not need to issue orders. You have to do what is even harder: find the still words that bring the storm.

For more on the transition from doer to leader of an organization, see *Doing Is Not Leading.* For more on the downside of a *"lion's voice,"* see *Leading Gently.* See also *Silent Killers* regarding Nietzsche's *"stillest hour,"* when the greatest events occur.

A Narrative from Mike Kail
EXECUTIVE TECHNOLOGIST, PALO ALTO STRATEGY GROUP

I started my technology career over 25 years ago at Control Data Systems, as a System Administrator. I was extremely introverted and my role felt comfortable. Servers and network gear don't require social interaction. Over a few years I developed a limited ability to push myself out of the comfort zone of silence, but I sometimes overcompensated and teetered on being a "brilliant asshole." Luckily a co-worker helped out, and we had several candid discussions about how to communicate more effectively and be more confident and assertive. For introverts, like me, who suffer from "Imposter Syndrome," those traits don't come naturally and require an inordinate amount of "social energy".

I progressed to Unix System Architect and was content and comfortable in that role. I could let my technical prowess do the talking and spend my time isolated in my own shell (pun intended). However, in this role I was always on-call, which meant that I would get paged about outages at any hour of the day. It was manageable, but I distinctly remember having an internal conversation around: "You're going to wake up someday, be in your 50s, and still be on-call. That's not what you aspire to."

The problem was that I had no experience in managing people, and given my introversion, the thought of that scared the hell out of me. Nevertheless, intrinsic motivation is a powerful force when channeled properly. In talking to other introverts over the years, I found it to be a common trait. I was now determined to take proactive steps to steer my career toward roles that offered more responsibility as well as opportunities to evolve.

I applied for a Director-level role at an early stage startup, and was disappointed and shocked when I got an email saying that they were passing. I had never experienced that before. Maniacal persistence is another trait of introverts, and when I discovered that the position was still not filled after a couple of months, I sent one of their C-Level executives a simple, but direct, email message stating that I felt that they had made a grave mistake, and that I was the proper person for the role. I got the job. Consistent with the Gandhi line above, this gentle but assertive effort "shook my world" and established a more confident foothold for my future.

During this time I began having aspirations to become a CIO. The startup didn't work out, and a close friend convinced me to join his company, where he was the CTO. My technical experience was well suited, and thanks to his ongoing mentorship, I grew a lot. I was now VP of IT for a company with offices in the Bay Area, Salt Lake City, and Germany. This "mash up" of cultures helped me evolve further out of introversion. I felt increasingly confident about my "social" abilities, and worked to develop some business acumen.

Though I considered my CIO aspirations "irrational exuberance," good luck arrived and I joined Netflix as its Director of Employee Technology. Imposter Syndrome reared its head: Netflix had massive talent density and I often felt like the weakest of the pack. I strived to work on some weaknesses, and among other things I started speaking at CIO events. Given my background as a distance runner, I have a reasonably high pain threshold, and I knew how to use mental games to push through a hard race. I used these same abilities during events and meetings where I was a focal point and there was no "escape." I was promoted to VP within a few months.

After 3.5 years at Netflix, I was asked to meet with Marissa Mayer, then CEO of Yahoo!, about a CIO role. I was flattered and beyond nervous. It helped that my "interview" was on a Saturday afternoon in her back-yard, removing the pressure of a corporate setting. Always the Imposter, I thought the 2.5 hour discussion went "ok," but when I checked my email that evening I was shocked to find a preliminary offer letter.

The next day was intense as I met with four senior executives and had to be "on" for about nine hours. It was both thrilling and draining and my mind raced with questions, concerns, excitement, and, of course, self-doubt. They made the offer official that evening, and after a sleepless night of conferring with my wife and mentors, I accepted the next morning. My first assignment was meeting with the PR team and conducting several press interviews. I could not have even imagined this sequence of events back when my primary interactions were with Unix.

To Nietzsche's advice I would add a line from Sun Tzu's Art of War: *"He who knows when he can fight and when he cannot, will be victorious."*

TACTICS

W hile *entrepreneurship* is full of interesting concepts, one must never forget the importance of *tactics*. You do have to get stuff done, after all, if you wish to *disrupt* anything. Though Nietzsche was a philosopher, many of his aphorisms relate to how to do things, drawing from his observations of human nature and psychology. Whether it is showing rather than telling, engaging your audience fully, or setting up the environment effectively in advance of communicating, Nietzsche understood how great performers get their message across.

"*Transparency*" is now an overused word, but Nietzsche knew the power of transparency in communication, especially when the real secrets are much more profound than what is on the surface. Weaving emotion into your communication, both to focus people and to draw them closer to you, can be powerful, but also harmful if misused.

To have perspective and situational awareness, you must do more than just work hard. Understanding how to step back, reflect on situations, and maintain a consistent intensity without burning out is another set of delightful ideas that appear in Nietzsche's writing.

On the surface, some of this might not feel like tactics. As you read Nietzsche's quote and consider what we have written about it, cycle back to the title of the chapter. If it now feels more tactical, how are you applying it in your business?

ONCE MORE
WITH FEELING

"The more abstract the truth you wish to teach,
the more must you allure the senses to it."

*In other words: To communicate abstract ideas
you need to trigger a sensory experience.*

As a leader, you often think abstractly about your business and organization. To build and grow, you must consider strategy, markets, and teams, not just particular features, customers, and individual employees. Often, you make decisions by applying generalizations or rules of thumb.

When you attempt to communicate these ideas to your team, customers, or investors, you should ensure that you capture the full scope. Look at your mission statement or statement of company values: their phrasing is necessarily general and vague so that individuals can find guidance in a wide variety of circumstances.

198 • THE ENTREPRENEUR'S WEEKLY NIETZSCHE

This tendency toward abstraction has a number of difficulties. Abstract terms have more variation in meaning across different individuals. The meaning of "fairness" depends on your values, whereas the meaning of "merit," though still abstract, is narrower, especially in the context of a company.

Many individuals are disinclined or unable to effectively process abstract information. The Myers-Briggs personality profile, for example, distinguishes between "Intuiters" (N) and "Sensers" (S). The latter prefer to use concrete modes of thinking and communicating, while the former favor abstractions.

Abstract and general terms are rarely inspiring or motivational, even to those who understand what you mean. There is a certain sterility to them; to achieve generality, one must rinse away the blood and guts.

To solve these difficulties, reiterate any message you wish to communicate, not merely by repeating it endlessly, but by offering examples. As Nietzsche says, you must *allure the senses to it.*" The examples need to be as specific, visceral, and emotional as you can make them. Instead of just repeating that "quality is our top priority," talk about a particular customer and how quality affected their business. Words with narrow and widely agreed meanings are better than general terms.

Even better, show a photograph or a video of an individual employee of that customer, illustrating how the product helped or failed them. Sensory experiences such as video and audio, or even physical objects that people can touch, are better than mere words. If these experiences contain emotional content, that is the best of all. If the customer in the video is visibly excited or disappointed, this will convey the message to your team's hearts, not just their minds.

You must provide a variety of such examples in order to occupy more of the territory addressed by the general statement. Otherwise, you risk the opposite problem: with a small number of examples, each one carries too much significance. Variety also improves the likelihood that at least one of the examples resonates with each person hearing them. Another benefit is that you are not telling the same stories repeatedly, since people stop listening when you repeat stories too often. After you offer each example, repeat the general statement so that people make the connection. The combination of the general statement with varied examples is the most powerful approach.

For examples of the role of emotion in communication, see *Right Messages, Attracting Followers*, and *Gratitude*.

A Narrative from Nicole Glaros
CHIEF INVESTMENT STRATEGY OFFICER, TECHSTARS

People see thousands of advertisements each year; the ads tend to blend together and the brain tunes them out. A similar effect happens to investors. They hear hundreds or even thousands of pitches a year, and those pitches all start to sound the same after a while. This makes it difficult for them to hear the real business opportunity. It is a significant problem for entrepreneurs who are trying to raise money.

One technique for battling this challenge is to use emotion to drive engagement with a pitch. At Techstars we call the technique "twist the knife." Do you see what we did there? Just a little, you felt or saw a knife being twisted – it is a little unsettling, but it got your attention better than the plain factual description. I've been teaching this technique to founders for the past ten years. The idea is to help an investor feel the customer's pain, or to have some other visceral or sensory experience, to engage them more with the pitch. It elevates their attention level above other pitches, and thereby increases the startup's chance of getting funding. Twisting the knife in just the right way can be a very effective way of closing capital.

In 2010 I worked with a company called Scriptpad that leveraged this technique extremely well. They could have simply told investors "Scriptpad is a service for doctors to send digital prescriptions to pharmacies." However, the listener doesn't feel the real opportunity with this purely factual description. What Scriptpad actually said was:

Scriptpad transforms the iPhone and iPad into a digital prescription pad, enabling doctors to write prescriptions faster and safer than their current paper process.

Why do this? Because the current process kills people.

Here is an example of a completely illegible handwritten paper prescription. [pitch includes a photo of a prescription] The pharmacist in this case dispensed the wrong heart medication because he couldn't read the doctor's handwriting. He mistook Isordil for Plendil, and instead of controlling the patient's condition, the medication caused a massive and fatal heart attack. And this happens again and again and again. [pitch includes a photo of many prescriptions] In fact, in the 1.7 billion handwritten paper prescriptions scrawled out each year on those familiar paper script pads, up to 40% contain some form of error, whether it's missed drug interactions, improper dosing, or just plain unreadable handwriting. Each year, 7,000 people die, and another million and a half are injured as a result of these errors, causing billions in hospitalizations and treatment costs.

After reading that, aren't you afraid to ever get a paper prescription again? Don't you feel like this service needs to exist for people's safety? Imagine: that illegible handwriting could actually kill someone! Scriptpad used a real example to highlight the emotion. They carefully chose words like safer, illegible, kills, fatal, familiar, scrawled *to draw emotional and sensory experience into their sentences.*

Now, Scriptpad used fear as their emotional driver, but any emotion can work. Joy, curiosity, affection, sadness – most emotions can help draw people into the story.

Leveraging just the right amount of emotion can be tricky, though. I frequently see pitches that err on the side of too much *emotion. For example, another company I worked with offered a service to help locate missing children. Early versions of their presentation showed a photo of a child, followed by a news photo of that child's body under a sheet, where it was found after the child was abducted. The presenter instructed you to imagine this happening to your own child. People hearing the pitch, including me, completely shut down at that point. It was too horrific to imagine. People looked away from the screen, and ultimately the company – the imagery and words were too close to home and they didn't want to engage.*

They revised and simplified the pitch to say "I started this company because a kid in my neighborhood went missing, and I don't want that to happen to any other kids." This had the right effect and people become more interested. It can take some practice and testing to get the balance right.

PLAY TO THE AUDIENCE

"It is not sufficient to know how to play well; one must also know how to secure a good hearing. A violin in the hand of the greatest master gives only a little squeak when the place where it is heard is too large; the master may then be mistaken for any bungler."

In other words: Performing well is not enough; the audience must experience the performance well. If the venue has bad acoustics, even a great violinist sounds terrible. A virtuoso can be mistaken for a novice.

Empathy, which is the ability to put yourself in someone else's shoes, is an important entrepreneurial skill. This comes into play in many types of circumstances, including when "someone else" is an entire audience. Whether you are speaking on a conference call, making an investor presentation, or sitting on a panel at a conference, to be effective, you should consider the perspective and context of the audience.

Audience empathy begins with asking whether the audience can literally hear and understand you. The difficulty is particularly acute with remote communication. Cell phone and Internet video conference connection quality is variable and sometimes poor. There is often a great deal of noise in the background, such as airport announcements or street sounds. While you might see this as a reality of contemporary business, an investor or customer on the other end probably does not care. She will be unimpressed because she did not understand much of what you said.

Whether on the phone or in person, if you have an accent (relative to your audience) or tend to talk fast or mumble, the same difficulty arises. The audience may have to work so hard to understand your individual words that they miss the gist of what you are trying to say and why it is important. People are busy and have a vast amount of information coming at them. If it is not easy to understand you, they will simply move on.

Beyond these brute mechanics, there is also the style of your presentation. Do you grab the audience's attention by addressing topics specifically of concern to them? Do you hold their attention by speaking with appropriate enthusiasm or by engaging them interactively? Do you annoy them by being too enthusiastic? Do you give any attention to your body language or appearance? Have you thought about who will be in the audience and what sort of style is best suited to their preferences? Do you give a presentation the same way every time, or do you customize it?

You have heard the cliché that you should know your audience. But equally important is what you do with that knowledge. Always make sure that they can hear and understand you clearly. Put energy into customizing your communication style to fit the audience, their interests, and their preferences.

For more on getting your message across in the right way, see *Right Messages*, *Leading Gently*, and *Once More with Feeling*.

A Narrative from Ben Casnocha

CO-FOUNDER AND PARTNER, VILLAGE GLOBAL AND
CO-AUTHOR OF *THE STARTUP OF YOU* AND *THE ALLIANCE*

In 2001 I founded one of my first companies, an enterprise software firm that sold customer relationship management tools to local governments. Delivering software via the cloud was new to these agencies. I was convinced that the novelty of our technology solution required at least a ninety-minute meeting to explain – nothing less. Once in the office of a government manager, I would spend the full ninety minutes talking at the prospect and demonstrating our software. At the very end, I would ask for any questions or comments.

After dozens of "thanks but no thanks" responses, I began to notice the glazed eyes and restless body language in my sales prospects, and realized what was happening. Even otherwise-interested people were tuning out after ten or fifteen minutes. As a first-time salesperson, I learned that to communicate effectively means you have to continuously earn the privilege of an audience's attention. An audience needs a good reason to stay engaged. They don't want to be talked at. Their attention span gives way.

Today, I give a couple of speeches a month about talent management. Attention spans have grown even shorter over the fifteen years since I started my software company, and audience engagement has become an even more important factor in effective communication. One way that I address this issue is by requesting lightweight audience participation.

For example, instead of simply sharing a theory for why most employees have terrible day-one experiences at their new job, I'll ask my audience to reflect: "Imagine it's your first day on a new job and your hiring manager walks in the room..." Or, instead of rattling off statistics about average employee tenure inside companies, I'll say: "Show me with your fingers how many years you've been at your current job." Then I connect what I learn from the "body poll" of the audience into the broader point I'm trying to make.

Be it onstage in a formal speech, or when leading any type of business meeting, I try not to let more than five or ten minutes pass without asking the people in a room to imagine a scenario, reflect on a situation, answer a question live in the room, or take a body poll with their fingers. These simple devices help maintain audience attention, which is essential to their hearing my message.

SHOW THE VALUE

> "We estimate services rendered to us according to the value set on them by those who render them, not according to the value they have for us."

In other words: We perceive the value of a service based on how the vendor presents it to us, not the actual value it brings us.

Customers do not necessarily behave rationally. Pricing, positioning, and customer experience are areas where it is crucial to be aware of your company's influence on customer perceptions.

If you underprice your product or service, even if it is to compete, you are telling your customers that it is a commodity. If you are too willing to negotiate on price, you are telling your customers that you are not confident in the value you will deliver. Most importantly, *you* need to have a sense of how much value you think the customer will gain. Your pricing should reflect that estimated value. It should not be based on the cost of providing the product or service, or on the prices inferior competitors charge.

Positioning your products as "strategic" or a "solution" is an example of this approach. Show your prospects a vision for how your products solve an entire problem or transform an outdated way of operating. A big vision creates excitement and enthusiasm. It shows that you see value in your products, value that greatly exceeds the immediate tactical functions they serve. This is a kind of leadership that helps customers think bigger and see a brighter future by using your products.

A similar analysis applies to customer experience. Fine restaurants know this well. They train servers to ask whether the food is "delicious," not whether everything is "OK." Your team must strike a balance between arrogance and confidence, but they should project a basic assumption that the company is providing great value. Starting with that assumption allows the customer to indicate dissatisfaction, but in a context where they understand that their delight was your company's objective. It also helps customers to perceive difficulties with the product or service in relation to the overall value delivered. Otherwise they may focus on problems as the most notable aspect of their experience.

Emphasize the value you are delivering to your customers by communicating it through value-based pricing, product positioning that offers a strategic vision, and customer service that assumes customers should have a great experience.

For ideas on how emphasis on value can be part of your company culture, see *Style*. For more on making sure the value is genuine, see *Domination*.

A Narrative from Sal Carcia

CO-FOUNDER AND SVP MARKETING & SALES, VIEWLOGIC SYSTEMS

In the early 1980s, I attended a presentation by one of the founders of Mentor Graphics, a successful electronics Computer-Aided Engineering

(CAE) company whose software ran on a high-power/high-cost graphics workstation called Apollo.

Mentor's pitch was centered on the engineer's workday, which was evenly divided between design, documentation, and communications. CAE products typically offered schematic drawing editors and logic and analog simulators for design, net- and part-lists creation for documentation, and file transfer capabilities for communications. The workstation platform offered generic word processors and email for other forms of documentation and communication.

The flaw was that the combined Apollo / Mentor workstation was so expensive that it was treated as a shared resource among the engineers. So it was not used for anything except the core functions, and tools like word processing and email were not used.

This was where the original idea for Viewlogic Systems came from. We targeted an IBM-PC (and compatible) platform, which was much less expensive than an Apollo. The workday concept made more sense on a PC because the system would reside on the engineer's desktop 24 hours a day, versus a centrally-located workstation.

Besides the standard design, documentation, and communications products, Viewlogic also offered its own integrated word processor (ViewDoc) and email (ViewMail). Integrating with third-party tools was difficult in those days, and our uniqueness was the integration with the design tools. As an example, we could easily cut and paste a schematic drawing from ViewDraw into a ViewDoc document, and then email it through ViewMail.

At our initial product introduction with local technology press, our plan was to spend most of the time showing the standard design tools and then end with the cut, paste, and email capability. It is worth noting that ViewMail was not yet working and ViewDoc was buggy, so that part of the demonstration was actually rigged. The demo of the design tools was *going well with the press, but then our VP of Engineering opened ViewDoc, typed a description of the design, cut a schematic, and pasted it into the ViewDoc document. The crowd began to stir and there were some oohs and aahs. At first, I thought they were joking, but they were not. Then he emailed the document to another engineer, and when it was opened, the crowd started to applaud.*

The same kind of excitement was visible at our formal introduction at the Design Automation Conference (DAC) a few weeks later, despite our being placed in a back corner of the exhibition hall. The crowds kept growing, we were a hit, and we got our largest customer, Toshiba, at that show.

Six years later we were in buyout discussions with a very large CAE firm whose CEO was an icon in the industry. At one point he turned to me and said that he remembered our first DAC. His face lit up with excitement. He began to describe how the schematics were being cut, pasted, and emailed between the PCs as if it was magic.

Yet, a couple of years after the initial product introduction, we dropped the ViewDoc product. It was not being used much by our customers. It never really worked that well, but more importantly, the PC-based workstation was not being used as a desktop product – despite its lower cost, it was still a shared resource. Nevertheless, while it was available, most customers were happy to pay extra for ViewDoc.

The value behind ViewDoc and ViewMail turned out to be that they symbolized to engineering managers that a PC presented an opportunity to actually spend more time with the design. It also represented an opportunity to open up greater information flow between the designers and other departments. This was and is today a classic problem with product design. The integration of these tools represented a vision of the potential expanded use of a PC-based CAE workstation. Our design tools were exciting but not unique. ViewDoc and ViewMail integrated into the overall design platform was unique. It was also exciting to watch and gave the company flair.

Viewlogic went on to be highly successful, launched with an initial product that was exciting because of its vision and what it symbolized, but ultimately built on a more familiar set of capabilities that mostly replicated competitive offerings at lower total cost.

STRONG BELIEFS

> " When the strength of a belief is emphasized,
> we should conclude that it is difficult to
> prove and unlikely to be true. "

*In other words: When people highlight how strongly they believe
something, rather than the underlying logic and facts that
support their belief, then the belief is probably not justified.*

Many people are inclined to take others at their word. This feature of psychology is an important part of the glue holding our civilization together. In contrast, consider the disarray that has resulted from the rise of fake news combined with the cavalier skepticism in response.

Everyone has certain red flags or triggers that suggest skepticism. One knows to be cautious when buying a used car or in dealing with a known liar. Philosophers call these "defeaters" of the basic assumption that people tell the truth.

Is Nietzsche saying that confidence in a belief is such a red flag? Not exactly. Note that he qualifies it with *"emphasized."* The alarm appears when the person does not merely *have* confidence in their belief, but seems to need to emphasize or tout it. No one finds it necessary to talk about how sure they are that the sun will rise tomorrow.

Suppose someone thinks that Joe is the best candidate for a job. When asked why, she says, "I strongly believe he is the best." She might say it loudly or forcefully. In this case, one might have cause for suspicion. If someone has good reasons for a belief and can articulate them clearly, why would they emphasize how strongly they believe it?

The sensitivity of our skeptical trigger varies according to our familiarity with the individual stating the belief. There is a broad continuum of behaviors relating to confidence. Some people are uncomfortable stating opinions unless they are genuinely confident in them and may struggle when challenged even if they do have good reasons. For others, manipulation is a primary operational tactic, and they may use an expression of strong belief to intimidate others and railroad their agenda. This is often effective because many people do not have the skeptical reflex we are discussing here.

As a leader and entrepreneur, you should take account of this issue both as the recipient of opinions and the provider of them. As a recipient, you must be on the lookout for beliefs with their strength emphasized. Yet you must also be careful in how you go about challenging these beliefs. It may turn out that the speaker knows more than you. Strongly held beliefs tend to be resistant to change, so while you may decide not to adopt those beliefs yourself, challenging them directly may not have the desired effect. This can be true whether the individual expressing them is an employee, a customer, or an investor.

When you offer your own beliefs, and you have considerable confidence in them, be sure to include the reasons for that confidence, not just the fact of it. If expressing beliefs strongly is part of your leadership style, and you sometimes use it to disguise uncertainty or difficulty articulating reasons, you should be aware that among some people it will erode confidence over time. The best people will eventually see through it.

For other angles on strong beliefs, see *Persistence* and *Resolute Decisions*.

TRANSPARENCY

" Many a shrewd one did I find: he veiled his countenance
and made his water muddy, that no one might see
therethrough and thereunder. But precisely unto him
came the shrewder distrusters and nut-crackers: precisely
from him did they fish his best-concealed fish! But the
clear, the honest, the transparent—these are for me
the wisest silent ones: in them, so *profound* is the depth
that even the clearest water doth not—betray it. "

In other words: I encountered many shrewd players who hid their
emotions and spoke vaguely and misleadingly, so that no one could
figure out their motivations and plans. But this attracted even shrewder
people who trust no one and specialize in fishing out information:
these people managed to get the best-concealed secrets out of them!
For me, the wisest are those who are clear, honest, and transparent;
their secrets are profound and even clarity does not divulge them.

Nietzsche asserts that people who are secretive and mysterious see themselves as shrewd, but are actually naive. We see this in entrepreneurs who are reluctant to provide much information about their businesses. Sometimes this is because they are worried someone will copy their idea. Or it is an attempt to generate interest by being mysterious. Often it is some of each. This coy and cagey behavior can manifest as an insistence on non-disclosure or confidentiality agreements before any discussions take place. Like Nietzsche, we find this behavior naive, unhelpful, and ineffective.

In the current era of accelerators, entrepreneurship programs at universities, and startup weekends, someone somewhere is pursuing nearly every business idea imaginable. In *Do More Faster*, Tim Ferriss makes this point and asserts that "your idea is worthless" because what matters is execution.

If you are confident that no one else has thought of your idea before, then it may be too early. If no one else seems to be pursuing it, then it may have deep-seated obstacles to success. In that case, others have probably considered the idea and recognized the difficulty—or already tried it, failed, and evolved their thinking. Assuming you have identified a solution to the obstacles, those other teams would also have evaluated and discarded your solution. For these reasons, if your idea is genuinely unique in the market, that in itself is a kind of argument against it.

If merely explaining your business idea to someone else could seriously impair your opportunity, then your idea is not defensible. Eventually, you will have to disclose the idea publicly to sell your products. Just as important, as Matt Mullenweg says (also in *Do More Faster*), "usage is like oxygen for ideas." Secrecy inhibits usage of and feedback for your idea. If your business idea needs to be a secret, it's probably not a good business idea.

A truly disruptive business idea whose time has come usually solves a problem that is easy to understand, given some knowledge of the domain. The opportunity lies in the confluence of factors that make it possible now to disrupt an industry, when it was not previously possible. These factors may include changes in the industry or customer behavior. They may relate to unique technology or a fundamentally new market entry strategy that you have developed. Often, these changes occur on the shoulders of other recent technological innovations or market shifts. It is a complex synthesis that is explained, not revealed.

Or it may be one of those ideas that no one believes will work, until it does.

Either way, your assessment of the opportunity will likely be controversial. Few people will agree that it is workable. Of those, fewer still will have your obsession with it, knowing that it would mean committing to working on the idea for a long time. If there is anyone left to copy your idea, despite having the knowledge to see its value and enthusiasm for the market, they somehow failed to come up with that idea themselves. Are you really worried about them and their ability to compete with you?

Secrecy about your business idea signals inexperience, because experienced entrepreneurs know that execution matters more than ideas, that good ideas need exposure to garner usage and feedback, and that ideas no one else is pursuing will be viewed as opportunistically weak.

If you try to be mysterious, it will have the opposite effect with experienced investors, customers, and employees. They are Nietzsche's *"nut-crackers,"* who will see right through your ploy. You are trying to convey that you are keeping something valuable a secret, but what they anticipate is that you are hiding a lack of substance. Less experienced people might be taken in by this behavior, and you may be able to scratch out a living from it, but it's unlikely that you will build a scalable business that way.

There are situations where it might make sense to operate in stealth mode for a time, especially if you don't quite know what your business is ultimately going to be. You might have some hunches and preliminary technology but are in the midst of exploring the direction you want to pursue. In these cases, you do not want to publicize your plans, because they are likely to change, and this might confuse customers, investors, or employees. It's much easier to pivot when you have not put a public stake in the ground. Further, you do not want to share the dead ends that you explored in this process, because knowing them will save competitors time. When you finally reveal your business publicly, no one will know what avenues you explored and therefore will not know whether you vetted your publicly disclosed direction. If you choose to pursue stealth mode, when you do talk to people about your business, you should be forthright about the fact that its direction is tentative. You don't have a big secret; rather, you have not fully decided on your direction.

Within the broader context of the business idea and market opportunity, most good startups do have some sort of unique and clever approach that is not obvious. In the jargon of startups, this is sometimes called a "secret sauce" or "unfair competitive advantage." This is a different matter. You should not share the details of your unique process methods, algorithms, or that key potential partnership that you have not quite signed yet. Speak of these in general terms and make it clear that you think it provides a unique advantage. However, if you are talking to investors, make sure that this differentiator is genuine. They will eventually find out what you have, and if you overstated its importance or uniqueness, you will lose credibility with these investors. Learn to talk about your unique approach in a way that shows where it adds value without making it easier for someone to replicate.

In some cases, such as due diligence, it will be necessary to disclose these details. Such cases are narrow and occur near the end of a process, not at the beginning. Even so, be careful with intellectual property such as trade secrets and unfiled patents where you can lose your legal rights through mere disclosure. Experienced investors will understand why you cannot disclose this information and will not see it as a ploy.

Nietzsche says that he prefers people who are transparent and honest. If what they are doing is deep and important, this transparency will not "*betray it.*" For him, this could be true in relationships, in values, or in creative projects. Applied to business, it means that a disruptive idea that has real substance does not need to be protected by secrecy.

For more on the cost of misleading people, see *Trust*. For the inevitable downside of transparency, see *Imitators*. For more on finding good business ideas, see *Domination*, *Doing the Obvious*, and *Deviance*.

RED HOT

> " So cold, so icy, that one burns one's finger
> at the touch of him! Every hand that lays
> hold of him shrinks back!—And for that
> very reason many think him red-hot. "

In other words: Interactions with him are
upsetting, so everyone is afraid of him. That makes
other people think he must be amazing.

Most people feel drawn to famous or notable individuals. At a minimum, one is curious about how they got to where they are and what they are like. One grants them esteem and would find pleasure in meeting or associating with them. In the extreme case, one might hold them in awe or even bestow worship on them.

You need to remain rational when meeting or considering working with well-known people. On the favorable side, such people probably did not get where they are by being mediocre or uninteresting. They have probably done something valuable or important. They likely have knowledge that you would find useful. Even if not, they have undoubtedly had experiences from which you could learn. Association with such people can open doors for you and mitigate the natural skepticism of those who do not know you.

There are also negatives. People of high status may have achieved it by questionable methods. They may treat other people as mere means to their ends. They may be too busy and in too much demand to offer any value. They may be unapproachable. Their success may have been due primarily to luck, and they may not be aware of it. Their status may cause them to be arrogant or intolerable.

For many entrepreneurs, this often arises in meeting with investors. Investors have either made a lot of money or have access to it. They are usually well-known, at least within the entrepreneurial and technology communities. Many of these people are amazing, valuable to know, and honorable. But some are jerks, intellectually shallow, or even underhanded. You cannot tell which it is from watching how other people talk about them or respond to them. The fame and the access to capital is too often confused with value.

Make your own judgments on these and other people with a *"red-hot"* reputation. Consider the opinions of people whom you trust and who also know the person well. Ignore the popular opinion and the person's portrayal in the media. Treat such a person with respect and perhaps a little deference where appropriate, but do not assume that you want to work with them or that they would be an unqualified boon to you or your business.

For more on thinking for yourself with *"red-hot"* people, see *Finding My Way* and *Monsters*.

A Narrative from Tracy Lawrence
CEO AND CO-FOUNDER, CHEWSE

I was raising money for my startup, Chewse, and we had sixty days until bankruptcy. I was in the middle of a rocky financing process and started to fear the worst.

In the midst of this fear, I was introduced to an investor whom a fellow entrepreneur adored. This investor was the lead partner at a well-known and respected firm, and I had had several positive interactions previously with one of the other partners.

As they got to know our company, I had the opportunity to talk to another partner at the firm. We had an incredibly candid conversation about my trials as a female founder. He opened up about his sympathies and expressed support. I was floored that a firm that was so well-known was also so willing to be vulnerable.

After many calls regarding the business model and customer references, we set a date for the lead partner to come visit the office and the team. This is usually a great sign that you're on track toward getting an investment.

The morning of the visit, he called me to break some news.

"I spoke to your customers, and they say that Chewse is one of the best services they use at work. Your growth is solid and the market is big."

I held my breath for the other shoe to drop.

"But, unfortunately, we don't have conviction in the team. This is a hard industry that's going to require a lot of blocking and tackling, and we don't think you're out for blood. We won't be investing in you."

I was in my little studio in San Francisco on the other end of that heart-breaking call and I felt smaller than ever. To have such a well-regarded investor tell me he lacked conviction in me caused me to crumble.

I thanked him for his time, hung up, and cried for half a day. I had to face some big questions:

Why would he think I'm not able to win in a fiercely tactical industry?

Is it because I'm a woman?

Am I too nice?

If a notable VC doesn't believe in me, why should I?

What the fuck am I doing in Silicon Valley?

The next day, I came to a realization. He was right.

I'm not out for blood. I don't look like my male counterparts in the industry. I'm out for love – and it's exactly this focus that makes our customers love us. It's also why we've attracted fantastic talent, restaurant partners, and investors.

IMITATORS

" A: 'What? You don't want to have imitators?' B: 'I
don't want people to do anything after me; I want
everyone to do something before himself (as a pattern
to himself)—just as I do.' A: 'Consequently—?' "

*In other words: A: You don't want people to copy your work?
B: I just don't want people to follow me. I want them to
create their own path. Like I do. A: And your point is?*

A text that Nietzsche intended to apply to creators in the arts, such as composers, painters, and poets, can also be applied to entrepreneurs, who are creators of products and companies.

There are many views on what constitutes ethical behavior in business and in entrepreneurship. In *Looking Out for #1*, Robert Ringer calls this the "line-drawing game." There are many different reasons people start companies: some want to make money, some want to make the world a better place, some seek power and fame, some want to create, and some just can't work for anyone else.

All these differences can lead to friction and confusion among people and companies. If you are by nature a creator, you may not understand why anyone would copy your work. If you are in it for the money, you may only care whether the copying is legal or what penalties you risk.

Competitors will copy you in both subtle and egregious ways. They might copy your products or their features, hire your employees or ex-employees to learn your sales tactics, or even use the same phrasing to describe their company and products. In a hot venture-funded market, even the fast-followers are targets for later entrants. Many people see this as a reasonable business strategy, and it serves to legitimize the market. You think everyone should be an original creator? So what? Not everyone sees it that way.

Don't expect others to share your values, ethics, or reasons for being in business. Don't be surprised when they actually live their own values, possibly at your expense. Awareness of differences like this is becoming more difficult in our echo-chamber cultural environment, but that awareness remains important for maintaining your perspective.

For more on the variety of ethical standards, see *Monsters*, *Trust*, and *Consequences*.

A Narrative from Jud Valeski
CO-FOUNDER AND CEO, GNIP

Gnip was first-to-market in its category, and we led that market through our acquisition by Twitter in 2014. Being first and leading the market seems ideal, but the challenges are severe. If the market opportunity is large, you have competitors constantly nipping at your heels and occasionally taking a bite.

We ran our company with a strong ethical emphasis, both internally and externally. While we would openly spar with competitors on occasion, it was always in a friendly manner. We believed the fight was in building the best product and delivering it to our customers, not in squabbling with the competition. I enjoyed my own naivety on this front, as it allowed me to feel righteous and clean. To me, building something via one's own merit is important, if not paramount, so I was shocked when I saw two patterns emerge in our competitors:

PATTERN #1: LINKEDIN TROLLING

As Gnip grew, we noticed our competition showing up more frequently in conversations with our customer prospects. I chalked it up to competition naturally getting more intense and real. However, a couple of colleagues had a different take – they noticed that my LinkedIn connections were all publicly accessible, and they asked me to make them private. They were suggesting that competitors were trolling my connections and using them as a map for their own business.

I've long been a LinkedIn member – since well before the robots took over the social graph – and I took seriously their early proposition of "only connect to people you really know." That spirit has been with me since. At Gnip I had continued making public connections on LinkedIn with prospective partners and customers. I disregarded my colleagues' fears as silly, and I reasoned that even if we were giving competitors a shortcut, they would find these prospects anyway.

Competition continued to increase; my colleagues' concerns about privatizing my connections grew louder and I eventually conceded. It then became clear that competitors had been walking through doors immediately after us, based on LinkedIn's cookie crumb trail. I couldn't believe someone would stoop so low as to use my connections instead of making their own.

I grew up a little in that moment; I became more jaded, more cautious. I realized that competitors were not merely fast-following our business idea, they were willing to pilfer the fruits of our effort in ways that I considered unethical and were in any case lacking in dignity.

PATTERN #2: CONTENT THEFT

Long after the war was effectively lost by our competitors, they continued to limp along like zombies. We noticed that they were starting to use, in their pitches and materials, marketing language and verbiage that we had created. Over time, the regularity and precision of this copying increased.

Some of this was expected, and even intentional, as we had created an annual industry conference where competitors were included. But we were able to pinpoint clear messaging and conceptual theft that went beyond the general ideas presented at the conference. I became convinced some of our competitors were unable to build their own plans, and were functioning purely as leeches.

My frustration peaked when our primary remaining competitor broadcast a live marketing podcast to discuss their product and company. I remember everything about the moment. I had scheduled my day so that I could be back in my hotel room with a reliable network connection, and some peace and quiet, to focus on the podcast. I sat on the edge of the bed and listened. Introductions were followed by a brief market setup and then a question to the competitor. It took a few sentences to hit me, but he was reciting or reading, verbatim, a talk I had recently given at a conference. I listened for another few minutes to confirm what I was hearing, and then closed my laptop.

It is inevitable that competitors and copycats will arise for any market-leading business. But don't underestimate how low they will stoop to compete.

STEPPING BACK

"When it is Necessary to Part.—You must, for a time
at least, part from that which you want to know
and measure. Only when you have left a city do you
see how high its towers rise above its houses."

*In other words: When you should get away: you must
occasionally get away from the things you want to
know and measure. You cannot see how high a city's
skyscrapers rise above the houses until you have left it.*

Nietzsche frequently emphasizes the idea of perspective: things look different from different vantage points. He sometimes goes further to suggest that there is no single privileged perspective on any matter. His message in this quote is simple: sometimes one must look at something from further away to see certain important aspects of it. We call this "stepping back."

In entrepreneurship, stepping back can take many forms, beginning with the trope of working on your business instead of working in it. This means looking at the business as a complete system and ignoring the particulars flowing through that system on a given day. You might think about the methods you use to find new customers or the methodology of your engineering organization. It might include reconsideration of your target market, assessing your company culture, or changing your organizational structure.

In most startups, an endless stream of daily fire drills preoccupies company leadership. There is always a human resources problem, urgent customer opportunity, or systems glitch that demands attention. Depending on the size of the company, it may be reasonable that such emergencies are a big part of your job. But they cannot be the entire job; otherwise, the company never improves, and growth will eventually expose flaws in its approach, often abruptly. Due to these everyday pressures, most entrepreneurs find that stepping back requires some sort of intentional and periodic effort.

Some companies accomplish this by holding founder or management team retreats. These do not need to be expensive boondoggles. You simply need to go somewhere different from the office, where the participants cannot be easily reached or distracted. Even a conference room at another company or a meeting room at a public library can work well. If you have appropriate funding, an overnight stay with associated team-building activities can be beneficial. Retreats can have other benefits, such as developing relationships among the leadership team in a different context and forcing the rest of the staff to solve problems on their own rather than leaning on management. Under this model, you literally *"part from that which you want to know and measure."*

Meeting with customers, vendors, or partners is another way to step back and gain a new perspective. Ask them to tell you what they think of your company, and listen carefully. Encourage them not to make it only about current issues and the direct relationship, although that will likely be where all their examples arise. You want to get their perspective as a trusted colleague. Or assemble a customer advisory board where you buy lunch for a half-dozen customers once a quarter and have them tell you what they think about your business.

In theory, it would be possible to do the same thing with employees, but often there are too many complications to obtain a helpful perspective directly. Their jobs depend on your view of them, and they may have an agenda unrelated to your goals for the company. Instead, do something simple, like observe the facial expressions of employees as they arrive at work in the morning and leave in the evening. Are they having fun? Do they look miserable?

One circumstance that can, but often does not, provide this sort of perspective is the Board of Directors meeting. You need to have a truly great Board for this to work, which includes Board members who are willing to study materials in advance, who do not use the meetings as an opportunity to promote their agenda or ego, and who are willing to focus on the meeting for a reasonable stretch of time. Few Board members meet all these criteria. You will often spend the meeting managing your Board instead of stepping back with them as partners and looking at the business from a new perspective. That said, it is worth trying to do this at least once with a given Board composition and expressing your desire for the Board to engage with you this way.

As the company grows, a culture of stepping back is helpful at all levels of the organization. This does not need to involve retreats and is often related to continuous improvement. For example, your company's engineering methodology might include debriefing after each sprint to discuss what worked and what didn't in the process, so that the team can adjust the process itself. Individual employees also need to self-improve and "Sharpen the Saw," as Stephen Covey puts it. You can use quarterly or annual reviews as an opportunity for employees to step back and see themselves from a new perspective. This only works if these reviews are separate from compensation reviews.

Consider stepping back with respect to measurement, as Nietzsche suggests. Most business metrics are a compromise: they provide insight into the operation in ways that do not create an excessive data collection or calculation burden. One measures what is easy to measure. This has become tempting with the availability of so much data about online behavior. But you need to regularly assess whether the information these metrics provide is useful or misleading relative to your business goals. Furthermore, there is a secondary effect with all metrics—you get what you measure. The metric's imperfect connection with business goals could mean that the presence of the metric leads away from your goals. A favorite example is purely revenue-based compensation for salespeople in organizations where they have control over deal variables that affect deal profitability. This will result in many unprofitable deals. You can mitigate such perverse effects by stepping back to look at your metrics from a safe distance.

Finally, all the day-to-day firefighting can sometimes make you feel like things are in shambles and instill negative attitudes in your team. Step back from your business and its details occasionally to review your progress over a longer period of time. This perspective will help you *"see how high its towers rise above its houses"* and give you renewed confidence.

For more on individual and organizational self-improvement, see *Surpassing*. For another example of an important rhythmic process in your business, see *Planning*.

SUSTAINING INTENSITY

"Where Danger is Greatest.—We seldom break our leg so long as life continues a toilsome upward climb. The danger comes when we begin to take things easily and choose the convenient paths."

In other words: The greatest danger: we rarely make big mistakes as long as we work hard and focus. It is when we reduce intensity and take shortcuts that problems arise.

Having spent a good deal of time hiking around Sils Maria, Switzerland, and other mountainous locations, Nietzsche was fond of analogies tied to mountains and climbing. The point expressed here is an actual rule of thumb among climbers: many injuries occur on the easier walk down after the completion of a technical ascent. While Nietzsche applies this guidance to life in general, one can also apply it to business.

When your entrepreneurial endeavor is new, you are aware that you have to pursue every reasonable opportunity and always be watching for threats. The threats come in many flavors: customer re-organizations, competitors receiving funding, an employee harassing others, or an undiscovered product flaw. You cannot afford to be caught unaware by any of these. The opportunities vary, and some require a strategic pivot to realize. The application of the adage does not mean putting blinders on and staying the course. Rather, it is about sustaining intensity, not maintaining direction. It seems only natural, after achieving a bit of success, to coast a little. Intense effort followed by rest makes sense and is more sustainable than unremitting intensity. Unfortunately, the world does not care that you want to relax. Its vagaries will manifest whether or not you are paying attention. Here are some scenarios:

> You have been working on a customer sale for a year, and finally, at the decisive meeting, the CEO says, "OK, let's move forward." You quickly turn your attention to other opportunities while you wait for the purchase order to come in. A month passes, and you learn that the CEO has stepped down.

> Your engineering team has delivered its last four iterations successfully and without major issues arising. To give them a nice break, you schedule the next system update for the Friday before Thanksgiving. "Murphy" takes note, and your service is unreliable during Black Friday and Cyber Monday, costing you dearly with customers.

> After three years, you have finally found product/market fit, and sales are growing rapidly. Every member of the management team is slammed trying to close deals, satisfy customer needs, and keep employees motivated. You cancel two leadership team retreats in a row because they just don't seem feasible or crucial. The intense

pressure within each function, combined with a lack of communication and connection, leads to passive-aggressive undermining between teams.

These scenarios may sound like bad luck or worst-case thinking, but they are the essence of business. Business is about making things happen, especially things that do not want to happen all on their own. You must shepherd them through to their conclusion, then continue to question whether they are really concluded or have merely reached a milestone on the way to their conclusion. You cannot take shortcuts unless you have thought through whether they will get you to the destination. As a Colorado sheriff once said, "if there was a safe shortcut [on Capitol Peak], it would be the standard route."

Andy Grove, in *Only the Paranoid Survive*, describes how this plays out at a strategic level and how to counteract it. If you are too late in detecting the "strategic inflection points" or "disruptive changes" in your business and industry, it can be fatal. This can happen at surprisingly early stages.

No matter how well things are going, do not assume that everything is just fine. Always keep your eyes open for things that might be going awry. Train your organization to think this way, and make it part of the culture. If an issue or area matters to the business, pursue it with unflagging intensity.

This approach can lead to burnout, and that risk merits attention. Another risk is that you become dismissive of success and never celebrate it. This is not a tradeoff or an inevitable consequence: you can celebrate a success without taking it for granted. Marking a new level can be simultaneous with envisioning the next one; follow up a good result with a discussion of how to repeat or even multiply it. Make this part of how your company celebrates, by treating a new plateau as a height from which you can see the next stage of the climb, not as a place to stop and rest.

For more on seeing change that might be coming your way, see *Two Kinds of Leaders* and *Seeing the Future*. For more on intensity over the long haul, see *Persistence*, *Patience in Disruption*, and *Obsession*.

CLEANING UP

"Moral for Builders.—We must remove the scaffolding when the house has been built."

In other words: Sometimes in construction one needs to build temporary structures to make the work easier. When construction is complete, remove these structures.

Almost any large project requires temporary infrastructure that will not be part of the finished product. Some of it is like scaffolding in that it is exterior to the product, such as concrete barriers in a road project. Some of it consists of low-quality components used as placeholders for the final ones, such as temporary stairs to enter a house under construction. You can think of both types of temporary infrastructure as "*scaffolding*."

Your startup has plenty of scaffolding, but there is often not an official project completion date by which you must remove it. There are some obvious milestones: for example, some types of legal and financial issues tend to be cleaned up prior to a first institutional financing round, and others when a company goes public. However, you will put new types of scaffolding into place at those times. Many technology products are in a continuous state of adding, fixing, and removing temporary measures. In a startup, you will add and remove the scaffolding as you go.

This is more difficult than it might seem. You may not realize that the way you are doing something today is, from tomorrow's perspective, a short-term solution. Even those things you initially see as temporary become familiar and habitual, and it becomes difficult to know when it is the right time to replace them. The default is to wait until a problem arises. However, being reactive can be detrimental to growth and results in perpetual firefighting.

Below, we describe a few common types of scaffolding that earlier-stage startups have and need to eventually remove. This will give you specific things to look for as well as ideas for other places to look. You should never view scaffolding as a mistake *per se*. If you had to do it to keep the business moving forward, then it was necessary at the time. But there is also a time to clean it up.

Business dealings with founders, family, and friends. Particularly in bootstrapped startups or those that start as family or lifestyle businesses, it is common for owners to lend money, personally guarantee debt, lease office space, or provide other services to the business. It is also common to work with family and friends as vendors. At a minimum, you should properly document these arrangements. Better, you should organize the business terms and procedures (especially the process for evaluating vendor renewals) so as to avoid conflicts of interest. In a high-growth startup, depending on the details, you may want to phase out these arrangements entirely.

Verbal agreements. Any undocumented understandings or strong expectations with investors, employees, vendors, or customers need to be either documented or eliminated.

Dead-weight founders and early employees. If people who helped the business get started are no longer helping to move it forward, you need to find ways to phase them out while treating them with respect and gratitude. One cannot overstate the negative cultural impact of keeping them around too long. Have a heart-to-heart conversation, help them find something new, and give them some extra vesting on their stock or stock options beyond their legal entitlement.

Over-reliance on founders. The opposite case is also common: startups tend to be heavily dependent on founders, along with their personalities and knowledge. This includes you—yes, you! Such reliance is necessary at first, and is fundamental to the company's early growth and cultural development, but eventually it can become risky and detrimental. A sustainable company and organization must rely on individuals, but most of the time it is better not to rely too heavily on any single person. The exception is when the leader is highly charismatic and gives rise to a cult of personality. Whether or not you are such a leader, a company that is too dependent on founders can be tricky to sell. Over time, build management, sales, and technical teams that can continue to carry the ball if something happens to you or one of the other founders.

Rickety financial systems. Most startups begin with QuickBooks or something similar and then start adding manual processes, spreadsheets, and miscellaneous databases to manage financial and management reporting and billing. This usually goes on too long, because everyone knows the heartache of implementing a comprehensive accounting system. If you wait until you hire a CFO to fix all this, you are probably waiting too long.

Technical debt. If you offer a technology-related product or service, you will always have technical debt—implementations that work for the moment but are not fully reliable, scalable, secure, or maintainable. Your technical staff is likely to constantly remind you of this, but it is easy to get into the habit of ignoring their pleading. This is especially acute if you have doctrinaire Agile product managers who see today's customer issues as always taking priority over the future. This is a tradeoff you need to continually evaluate.

For more on avoiding constant firefighting, see *Stepping Back*. For one idea on how to get things cleaned up, see *Integrators*.

CONCLUSION

By now you realize this book is not really about Nietzsche—it is about you and your business. Nietzsche's philosophy promotes thinking deeply, self-surpassing, creativity, and inspiration. We have attempted to use his unusual perspectives and clever phrasing as a way to convey some of these virtues.

We hope that the book has made you think. Entrepreneurship is a lively and often frantic activity. Yet there are benefits to stepping back regularly and thinking deeply, from a variety of perspectives, about what you are doing. This can help you solve problems that seem intractable and notice opportunities or risks that were not previously apparent. It can help ensure that you are on the right path—for you, or for your business, or both.

We hope that the book has helped you learn and grow. Entrepreneurship is a demanding and often thankless master. To be successful, you must continue to grow and improve, yet the job itself only provides for haphazard and painful learning opportunities. This book offers some substantive ideas that may add to your repertoire, but the umbrella idea of treating your own development and growth as part of the job and as central to your own and the company's success can last you a lifetime.

Finally, we hope that the book has inspired you. Entrepreneurship is a difficult and frequently lonely road. In facing your challenges, it is helpful to be aware and regularly reminded that what you do is important, difficult, valuable, and rare. It is also among the most fulfilling practical endeavors you can pursue.

APPENDIX I

NIETZSCHE'S LIFE AND LEGACY

Friedrich Nietzsche was born on October 15, 1844, in the tiny village of Röcken, on the outskirts of Leipzig, Germany. His father, Karl, was a Lutheran pastor whose own father had been both a pastor and a Protestant scholar. His mother, Franziska, also the child of a pastor, married Karl at age seventeen and gave birth to Friedrich a year later, followed by Elisabeth in 1846 and Ludwig in 1848.

In 1849, when Friedrich was only four, his father fell ill and died a few months later of a "brain ailment." Several months after that, his brother, Ludwig, age two, also died. Having lost the pastor's income and official home, the family moved fifteen miles west to Naumburg. The subsequent household of six included his mother, his father's mother and her two sisters, and his own sister—he was the only male. In little Röcken the family had been known and respected; here they were somewhat isolated.

"Fritz," as his family called him, was precocious, shy, and sickly. By age twelve, he had headaches and pain in his eyes. He did make two lifelong friends, Gustav Krug and Wilhelm Pinder, during his childhood and early adolescence. Through the families of these friends, he was introduced to serious literature and music and began to write music and poetry of his own. At school, he learned Greek and Latin and started to read the classics, as well as German greats such as Johann Wolfgang von Goethe.

At fourteen, Nietzsche entered Schulpforta, a prestigious Protestant boarding school a few miles from home, on a free-ride scholarship—due to his status as the son of a deceased pastor rather than his unimpressive grades. Nevertheless, he excelled there, adding Hebrew and French to his languages and becoming involved with the poetry of Friedrich Hölderlin and the music of Richard Wagner. He also read David Strauss's *Life of Jesus, Critically Examined*, which initiated the process of Nietzsche losing his Christian faith.

His performance at Schulpforta earned him a spot at the University of Bonn, where he enrolled in 1864 at the age of nineteen. He began with a concentration in theology and philology (the study of classics) with the intention of becoming a minister. He joined a fraternity called *Franconia*, continued to read works of Christian doubt, and after one semester, lost his faith entirely. This created considerable and lasting difficulties in his relationship with his devout mother and sister.

After one year at Bonn, Nietzsche followed his favorite professor, Friedrich Ritschl, to the University of Leipzig to study philology. There he published his first essays, discussing certain pre-Socratic Greek philosophers as well as Aristotle. In his first year at Leipzig, he discovered the work of Arthur Schopenhauer, an atheist successor to Immanuel Kant who emphasized aesthetics and music. Though Nietzsche later found many things to disagree with in Schopenhauer, he embraced the philosophy, and its influence on his thought—and his relationships—was significant. In his second year, he read Friedrich Lange's *History of Materialism*, which introduced him to Darwin's theory of evolution.

In 1867, he signed up for a year of military service, with promising prospects, but was injured on horseback after six months. The injury resulted in infections and other complications; attempts to combat them resulted in digestive problems that would plague him the rest of his life, adding to the misery of his headaches and eye pain. During both his service and recovery, he lived at home in Naumburg and had the opportunity for serious reading and writing. He returned to Leipzig just long enough to complete the equivalent of his undergraduate degree.

Two crucial turning points occurred in 1868. First, he met composer Richard Wagner, who became a friend, father figure, and aesthetic inspiration for the next decade. They shared an interest in Schopenhauer, and Nietzsche was deeply engaged with Wagner's theories of art, which at the time were driving the composer's ongoing creation of the *Ring* cycle of operas. Second, Professor Ritschl and others recommended Nietzche for a faculty post in philology at the University of Basel, which was offered to and accepted by Nietzsche. At the age of twenty-four, he became their youngest classics professor ever, without completing a doctorate.

1869, a young professor at Basel

In accepting the position, he renounced his Prussian citizenship and became legally stateless for the rest of his life. As a professor, he applied himself diligently to both teaching and research. He was granted tenure and a raise after only one year. Nevertheless, he became progressively disillusioned with the methods and milieu of the field of classics. In 1870, despite his citizenship status, he served as an ambulance driver in the Franco-Prussian War and managed to contract both diphtheria and dysentery, further worsening his health. During this time, he visited Wagner as much as possible and also developed a close relationship with Wagner's wife, Cosima, the daughter of Franz Liszt.

Nietzsche's first book, *The Birth of Tragedy from the Spirit of Music*, was published early in 1872. It was neither a commercial nor a critical success. While the book is ostensibly about classical Greek tragedy, it emphasizes culture and philosophy. It reflects Nietzsche's distaste for the political and cultural direction in which Germany and Prussia were headed, and it demonstrates his creative impulses in a field that was stodgy and dry. Wagner's views on art and music are apparent throughout. Years later he wrote a preface to a new edition of the book that partially disavowed it. Yet the Apollonian/Dionysian distinction and other elements introduced in the book had a considerable impact on 20th-century arts and culture.

1875, near the end of his active professorship

His second book, *Thoughts out of Season*, was published in parts from 1872 to 1876. It covers a variety of topics, cementing his intellectual transition away from philology and toward philosophical and cultural issues. It shows a continuing strong influence of Schopenhauer and Wagner. The latter had moved to Bayreuth to establish the famed music festival (active to this day) highlighting *The Ring* and his other works. Things were never quite the same between Wagner and Nietzsche after that move, though they continued to have a relationship for a number of years.

Nietzsche's health and vision continued to decline, and he would have spells, lasting for days, of partial blindness, fever, and bodily fluids emitting from both ends. He took frequent and increasing leaves of absence from his post at the University of Basel, culminating in his resignation with a pension in 1879. Due to his bad vision, he wore dark glasses and often needed a friend or assistant to take dictation in order to write his books.

From 1878 to 1883, Nietzsche's so-called middle-period, he published four books: *Human, All-Too-Human*; *The Dawn of Day*; *The Joyful Wisdom*; and *Thus Spoke Zarathustra*. The first three are aphoristic, with sections ranging from a single line to a couple of pages, and provide the first introductions to many of his philosophical ideas. *Zarathustra* is completely different. It is a work of fiction with elements of prose poetry, mystical settings, a high density of allusion, and leitmotifs reminiscent of *The Ring*. To the extent that Nietzsche's recommended response to the specter of nihilism is art, *Zarathustra* is his contribution and his illustration of that principle.

With his resignation from the university, Nietzsche began a somewhat nomadic life that would last through the remainder of his productive years. He spent summers in Sils Maria, Switzerland, winters in various Italian locales, and occasionally spent time in Naumburg with his family. In 1882 in Rome, he met Lou Andreas-Salomé through his friend Paul Rée. Salomé was young, brilliant, beautiful, and rebellious;

1882, amid his productive "middle period"

Nietzsche fell in love and proposed marriage.

Unfortunately, her plan was for a love triangle and intellectual commune with Nietzsche and Rée, which did not suit Nietzsche. His mother and sister did not care for Salomé and her libertine attitudes and did what they could to subvert the relationship. Eventually, Salomé and Rée went their own way. Nietzsche was greatly isolated at this time: he lost both a close friend and a love interest, was alienated from his family, and soon learned of the death of Wagner. It is in this emotional context that he began to write *Thus Spoke Zarathustra*.

At this point, Nietzsche entered a phase of declining health and intensifying productivity. Often he had help from friends, who read to him and transcribed his manuscripts. He augmented several of his previous books, published *Beyond Good and Evil* in 1886, and followed it with *The Genealogy of Morals* in 1887. In 1886–87 he began a project called "The Will to Power" but abandoned it as a chaotic jumble of notes. In 1888, he published five shorter books, the last of which was *Ecce Homo*, an autobiography.

On January 3, 1889, he suffered a complete mental collapse and was an invalid for the rest of his life, cared for initially by his mother and later his sister. There is evidence in his letters and in *Ecce Homo* that his mental health had been increasingly unstable toward the end of

1888; some who knew him thought it had been deteriorating for quite some time. There is no definitive diagnosis of the cause. At one time it was thought to have been syphilis. It could also have been inherited from his father, resulted from some of the drugs he took to combat his other health problems, or indicated a brain tumor. In the small favors department, his physical health problems abated considerably, and he was probably not in pain. He lived in this state for another decade, unaware of his growing fame, and died on August 25, 1900, at age fifty-five.

Nietzsche's sister, Elisabeth Förster-Nietzsche, was his heir and the curator of his works during his final years and after his death. Elisabeth's own life is fascinating in its own right, and though we will not go into it here, we observe that mental instability can take many forms. She assembled and edited a book called *The Will to Power* from Nietzsche's notes, some of which were no more than scribbles, and published a complete edition in 1906. It is normally not considered among Nietzsche's definitive works and is surely not the *magnum opus* that Elisabeth promoted it as.

Nietzsche sold few books prior to his mental collapse, numbering perhaps in the low thousands. He and his publisher eventually parted ways, and he had to use his meager savings and pension to have his later books printed. In 1888, a series of lectures given

Elisabeth Förster-Nietzsche

by Georg Brandes, a prominent European critic, changed everything. Calling Nietzsche's philosophy an "aristocratic radicalism," Brandes introduced Nietzsche to the world as an important thinker. Nietzsche was aware of this turn of events and wrote to Brandes in approval of the terminology. But his mental capacities did not survive to see the rapid growth of his fame and influence that transpired during the last decade of his life.

The diagram below attempts to capture a sort of genealogy of intellectual predecessors who influenced Nietzsche and successors whom he influenced. Nietzsche did not merely elaborate on or repair the ideas of his predecessors and then pass them on to his successors for further refinement. Instead, he synthesized entirely novel notions that resulted in complex, diverse, and diffuse influences. His thought interacted with a variety of fields and was not limited to "philosophy" in a traditional sense.

Understanding the details of this flow would require an elaboration of Nietzsche's thought that goes far beyond the scope of this book. However, let's illustrate how it works with an example.

"Perspectivism" is the idea that every view on every topic arises from some particular perspective and, crucially, that a "view from nowhere" that is entirely objective does not exist at all. Instead, the concepts with which one organizes the world are an "illusion"; they have utility but not truth. We rely on this idea in the chapter *Finding Your Way*.

For Nietzsche, perspectivism is in part an outgrowth of the influence of Schopenhauer, who elaborated and modified the work of Kant, who in turn had the insight that our individual minds are active participants in organizing our experience of reality. Nietzsche's distaste for Socrates (through the writings of Plato), who saw universal forms as underlying all reality, reinforced the notion. Darwin's theory of evolution dispensed with the idea of permanent and definitive natural

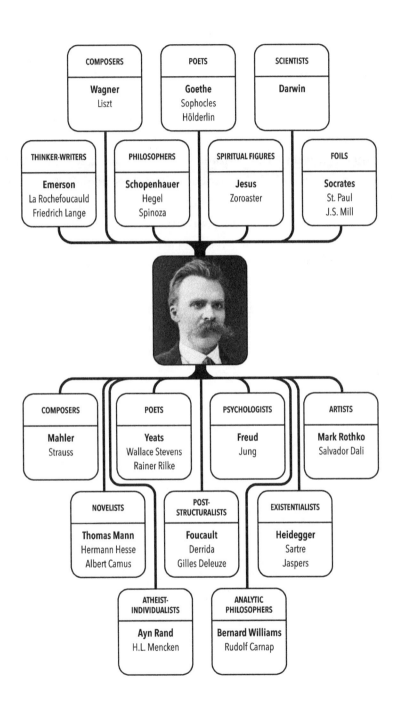

COMPOSERS	POETS	SCIENTISTS
Wagner Liszt	**Goethe** Sophocles Hölderlin	**Darwin**

THINKER-WRITERS	PHILOSOPHERS	SPIRITUAL FIGURES	FOILS
Emerson La Rochefoucauld Friedrich Lange	**Schopenhauer** Hegel Spinoza	**Jesus** Zoroaster	**Socrates** St. Paul J.S. Mill

COMPOSERS	POETS	PSYCHOLOGISTS	ARTISTS
Mahler Strauss	**Yeats** Wallace Stevens Rainer Rilke	**Freud** Jung	**Mark Rothko** Salvador Dali

NOVELISTS	POST-STRUCTURALISTS	EXISTENTIALISTS
Thomas Mann Hermann Hesse Albert Camus	**Foucault** Derrida Gilles Deleuze	**Heidegger** Sartre Jaspers

ATHEIST-INDIVIDUALISTS	ANALYTIC PHILOSOPHERS
Ayn Rand H.L. Mencken	**Bernard Williams** Rudolf Carnap

kinds (species) and Hegel's dialectic played a similar role in historical analysis. Despite similarities, most scholars do not think perspectivism amounts to relativism.

If you are familiar with existentialism or post-structuralism, you can imagine how perspectivism might have influenced those thinkers. Martin Heidegger's characterization of "human being," called Dasein, is fundamentally a kind of perspective along these lines. Poet Wallace Stevens is notoriously challenging to interpret, but some critics have argued that several of his poems contain direct expressions of perspectivism. Bernard Williams relies on perspectivism to argue against both moral realism and simplistic notions of truth extant in analytic philosophy.

While none of these patterns of influence are important for understanding the book, our hope is for a future version of this diagram to contain the category "Entrepreneurs" on the bottom, with your name listed.

DON'T BELIEVE EVERYTHING YOU HEAR ABOUT NIETZSCHE

INTRODUCTION: THE CHALLENGE OF INTERPRETING NIETZSCHE

Most people have heard or read something about Nietzsche or his philosophy that they find discomfiting. For example, you might have read that he was associated with the Nazis or that his notion of the overhuman (sometimes translated "superman") was advocacy for eugenics. In this essay, we aim to ease concerns you might have. Hopefully, you can then breathe easier when you hear of someone you find abhorrent claiming an affinity for Nietzsche. It is not at all required reading for understanding the book, although you may find that it provides useful background. You will also find this essay to be considerably more academic in style than the rest of the book, apropos its subject matter.[1]

We will not be able to demonstrate definitively whether Nietzsche held any particular substantive view. Scholars have debated these questions since they began reading Nietzsche in the 1890s, and while there is some agreement on certain points, there is little overall consensus. We are not Nietzsche scholars or experts and do not intend to enter that fray. Instead, what we aim to do is show you that—and why—strong claims about Nietzsche's philosophy, particularly as they relate to politics, are suspect.

Our first piece of evidence is the sheer breadth of thinkers and activists who have been heavily influenced by his work. For example, Nietzsche was a major influence on Zionists Theodor Herzl and Martin Buber; poets W.B. Yeats and Wallace Stevens; philosophers Jean-Paul Sartre (who was politically a Marxist) and Martin Heidegger (who was arguably a Nazi); psychoanalysts Sigmund Freud and Carl Jung; libertarian novelist-philosopher Ayn Rand; leftist post-structuralists like Gilles Deleuze and Jacques Derrida; and spiritualist Ken Wilber. Clearly, there is something in Nietzsche much deeper than any simple political or ethical view could explain. He was truly an original and disruptive thinker.

Nietzsche's writing style also creates difficulties in forming unambiguous conclusions. Some have argued that Nietzsche is actually a poet, and certainly his *Thus Spoke Zarathustra* is a kind of prose poem.

---

1   References to Nietzsche's works are presented by title, chapter, and section number rather than page number, since we rely on public domain sources online and on Kindle, where there are not always page numbers, and because the reader may wish to rely on a different translation or edition. The source translations for quotations in this essay are the same as those indicated in Appendix 3.

He is often sarcastic, which means that any given quote, taken out of context, might mean exactly the opposite of what he intends. His writing is often allegorical and allusive, so it not only requires interpretation but also knowledge of the prior works and thinkers to whom he may be referring (including, for just a few examples, the Bible, Sophocles, Plato, Shakespeare, Hölderlin, Schopenhauer, and Goethe—not exactly everyday fare). He wrote in German and was a fan of puns and neologisms, so accurate translation into other languages is challenging. His narratives and parables include characters who express points of view that he subsequently (though not always transparently) criticizes. His early works are structured as a set of aphorisms and short essays that are not necessarily connected or sequenced in an obvious fashion. These aphorisms rarely comprise a complete argument. Even when he makes direct statements, they are sometimes followed by an equally direct statement that says, in effect, "on the other hand." While his work is not utterly inscrutable, much of it is ambiguous and requires considerable effort to interpret. As lay readers, we have found that Nietzsche's work is much more effective at inspiring fresh thinking than it is at communicating clear positions.

These ambiguities and equivocations go well beyond style. An important element of Nietzsche's philosophical approach seems to be an anti-dogmatism applied broadly. In *Beyond Good and Evil*, he is fairly clear on this matter:

> *To speak seriously, there are good grounds for hoping that all dogmatizing in philosophy, the solemn air of finality it has given itself notwithstanding, may none the less have been no more than a noble childishness and tyronnism...*[2]

---

2   *Beyond Good and Evil*, Preface.

256 • THE ENTREPRENEUR'S WEEKLY NIETZSCHE

He does not spare himself: he often mentions that poets are liars, and he frequently follows his polemic outbursts with a sort of backtracking or even contradiction. Professor Kathleen Higgins, a Nietzsche scholar at the University of Texas, has argued that, in doing this, Nietzsche aims to show us what philosophizing is like, or how one should conduct it.[3] Later in *Beyond Good and Evil*, he writes "Granted that this also is only interpretation—and you will be eager enough to make this objection?—well, so much the better."[4] If this anti-dogmatic meta-philosophy is a reasonable reading of Nietzsche, then some combination of ignorance and mental gymnastics is required to use his work to justify dogmatic views such as Marxism or white nationalism.

Finally, Nietzsche left behind an extensive Nachlass (notes, letters, and unfinished manuscripts). Some of these writings, most notably the book *The Will to Power*, were edited, arranged, and published by his sister and guardian, Elisabeth Förster-Nietzsche, after his mental collapse in 1889. Given the difficulties of interpreting even his published works, it seems entirely fraught for anyone other than a dedicated Nietzsche scholar to put much emphasis on these unpublished fragments, at least in terms of ascribing a definitive point of view.

All this adds up to a situation where one could justify almost any interpretation of Nietzsche by cherry-picking bits of text and ignoring context. This is precisely what Elisabeth did in endearing herself and her brother's works to the nascent National Socialist Party in Germany, more than twenty years after Nietzsche's death. She and

---

3   Kathleen Higgins, "Thoughts That Come on Doves' Feet: Philosophy as Experience in the Work of Friedrich Nietzsche" (Franke Lectures in the Humanities, given at Yale University, November 7, 2013). Video available on YouTube.

4   *Beyond Good and Evil*, Chapter 1: Prejudices of Philosophers, section 22.

her husband, Bernhard Förster, were highly visible anti-Semitic pro-to-fascists.[5] Though Förster died in 1889 and (Friedrich) Nietzsche in 1900, Elisabeth lived until 1935 and joined the Nazi party. Adolf Hitler attended her funeral. Nietzsche scholar and translator Walter Kaufmann, in his 1950 book *Nietzsche: Philosopher, Psychologist, Antichrist*, details why one should disassociate Nietzsche's works and thought from this entire sordid enterprise.

At this point, we must admit that in this book, our own interpretations of Nietzsche's words are guilty of some amount of cherry-picking and context-dropping. We discuss this in the Introduction. For the purposes of this appendix, we simply note that our aim in the book—that you think differently and harder about your business and your career—is surely more innocuous than the extreme and vile philosophies we are concerned about here.

Thus far, we have addressed the idea that there are good reasons, in general, to be skeptical of strong claims about what Nietzsche believed and was trying to say. Now we will offer some specifics about views that may be of particular concern. As mentioned above, our goal is not to argue comprehensively, but merely to demonstrate that one can reasonably doubt claims that Nietzsche held these views.

ANTI-SEMITISM

Early in his career, Nietzsche was a friend and protégé of composer Richard Wagner. Wagner was quite successful and famous by this

---

5   See, for example, the article "The Search for the German Ideal," a version
    of which is published in the German-language *Journal of History* 6 (1994):
    485–496, outlining the endeavors of Bernhard Förster: http://users.utu.fi/
    hansalmi/forster.html.

time; he was also an early German proto-fascist and anti-Semite, evidenced by (among other things) his critical essay *Das Judenthum in der Musik* ("Jewishness in Music"). After a few years of idolization, Nietzsche fell out with Wagner for several reasons, among them the fact that he could not tolerate these views:

> *I took leave of Wagner in my soul. I cannot endure anything double-faced. Since Wagner had returned to Germany, he had condescended step by step to everything that I despise—even to anti-Semitism.*[6]

Nietzsche does criticize Jewish culture and values at times, but most of these criticisms are similar in nature to those he aims at Christianity. In particular, the Jews were, in his view, the initial creators of what he calls slave morality, at the time (3,000 or so years ago) when they were, in fact, slaves. He thinks this made sense for them as a survival mechanism at the time. The real travesty, for Nietzsche, is that this moral system became more widely embraced, via Christianity, to the extent that virtually everyone has adopted it to some degree. He sometimes also criticizes Jews for being too sheepish. These criticisms are sporadic and entirely unlike the sort of obsessive fear-mongering typical of anti-Semitic writers. In *The Dawn of Day*, one can see a typical example:

> *...the resourcefulness of the modern Jews, both in mind and soul, is extraordinary. Amongst all the inhabitants of Europe it is the Jews least of all who try to escape from any deep distress by recourse to drink or to suicide, as other less gifted people are so prone to do. Every Jew can find in the history of his own family and of his ancestors a*

---

6   *Nietzsche Contra Wagner*, "How I Got Rid of Wagner," section 1.

long record of instances of the greatest coolness and perseverance amid difficulties and dreadful situations, an artful cunning in fighting with misfortune and hazard. And above all it is their bravery under the cloak of wretched submission, their heroic spernere se sperni [*"to scorn the scorning of oneself"*] *that surpasses the virtues of all the saints.*[7]

Just as important, Nietzsche does not single out the Jews for this sort of stereotyping. He writes critically about culture, and he criticizes almost everyone he can think of: Christians, philosophers in general, and numerous specific philosophers, poets, Europeans, and Germans. His book *Twilight of the Idols* is, in part, a litany of these critiques.

GERMAN NATIONALISM

Born in Prussia (then a part of the German Confederation), Nietzsche was offered a professorship in Basel, Switzerland, at age twenty-five. When he moved there to accept the position, he renounced his Prussian citizenship and remained officially stateless for the rest of his life. He lived rather transiently in Switzerland, Italy, and France, though he did occasionally visit Germany. He often claimed a Polish heritage; the validity of that claim is controversial. If he was a German patriot or partisan, he had an odd way of going about it.

We will offer here a few of his words that suggest that his interest in politics was limited and that he was no fan of German nationalism. As discussed, one would have to assess the full context of these quotes to know whether ours is a correct interpretation; however, the words are clear enough to cast doubt on claims to the contrary.

---

7   *The Dawn of Day*, section 205.

In his autobiography, Nietzsche says, "I am perhaps more German than modern Germans—mere Imperial Germans—can hope to be,—I, the last anti-political German."[8] Across his works, he speaks frequently of the German people, but the emphasis is strongly on their culture, including philosophy, religion, morality, history, literature, music, language, and education. He has both negative and positive things to say; on balance he is critical of Germans in these domains, emphasizing decline from prior greatness. Importantly, he sees Germany's consolidation of geography and power as a cause of this decline, not the solution. He says:

> ...it is not only obvious that German culture is declining, but adequate reasons for this decline are not lacking. After all, nobody can spend more than he has:—this is true of individuals, it is also true of nations. If you spend your strength in acquiring power, or in politics on a large scale, or in economy, or in universal commerce, or in parliamentarism, or in military interests—if you dissipate the modicum of reason, of earnestness, of will, and of self-control that constitutes your nature in one particular fashion, you cannot dissipate it in another. Culture and the state—let no one be deceived on this point—are antagonists...[9]

He also delves into the cultural psychology of the German people, usually with an unflattering result. For example:

> A German is capable of great things, but he is unlikely to accomplish them, for he obeys whenever he can, as suits a naturally lazy intellect. If he is ever in the dangerous situation of having to stand alone and

---

8   *Ecce Homo*, "Why I Am So Wise," section 3.
9   *Twilight of the Idols*, "Things the Germans Lack," section 4.

cast aside his sloth, when he finds it no longer possible to disappear like a cipher in a number (in which respect he is far inferior to a Frenchman or an Englishman), he shows his true strength: then he becomes dangerous, evil, deep, and audacious...[10]

And again from his autobiography:

What is it that I have never forgiven Wagner? The fact that he condescended to the Germans—that he became a German Imperialist... Wherever Germany spreads, she ruins culture.[11]

Nietzsche's concern seems to be the negative impact on culture rather than the political implications of German imperialism. Only infrequently does he foray into the substance of German politics, and in these cases, he is consistently critical. For example, he includes this passage in a section that speaks of those who are politically homeless, as he is:

...we are not nearly "German" enough (in the sense in which the word "German" is current at present) to advocate nationalism and race-hatred, or take delight in the national heart-itch and blood-poisoning... We homeless ones are too diverse and mixed in race and descent as "modern men," and are consequently little tempted to participate in the falsified racial self-admiration and lewdness which at present display themselves in Germany, as signs of German sentiment, and which strike one as doubly false and unbecoming in the people with the "historical sense."[12]

---

10 *The Dawn of Day*, section 207.
11 *Ecce Homo*, "Why I Am So Clever," section 5.
12 *The Joyful Wisdom*, section 377.

While this selection of quotes is particularly succinct and telling, they seem to be representative of other elaborations in Nietzsche's works. One may feel a begrudging admiration for Elisabeth's ingenuity in managing to convince the Nazis that her brother's work is something they should be associated with.

WHITE NATIONALISM

Much has been made in the press in the past few years about an alleged resurgence of interest in Nietzsche among white nationalists and the "alt-right" in the United States. If you perform a Google search on Nietzsche, numerous articles of this nature are listed. We dug into this, and what we found was fascinating. Virtually all of these articles refer back to a single article in the *Atlantic*[13] about Richard Spencer, one of the leaders and originators of the "alt-right" and in our view a despicable individual. Few of the referring articles add any additional substance about a connection between Spencer and Nietzsche; instead, they either rehash the stories from Nazi Germany or emphasize the intellectual spuriousness of the connection.

Then we looked more closely at the *Atlantic* article mentioned. There is only one actual quote from Spencer that relates to Nietzsche. Spencer says, "You could say I was red-pilled[14] by Nietzsche," and the author goes on to suggest that this was a result of Spencer's reading *The Genealogy of Morals*. The article mentions an assortment of other disparate philosophers and writers. The photo of Spencer's "bookshelf" (we wonder: is this uncrowded decorative bookshelf intended

---

13 Graeme Wood, "His Kampf," *Atlantic*, June 2017.
14 A reference to the movie *The Matrix*, intending an epiphany about how the world secretly operates.

to demonstrate some irony in Spencer's new-found erudition?) shows a James Bond novel and a Batman book but nothing by Nietzsche, despite the caption.

An earlier *Mother Jones* article profiling Spencer[15] indicates that the "red-pill" experience came more from Spencer's reading of Jared Taylor, a self-described "white advocate." It does attribute a "lasting impression" on Spencer from Nietzsche, primarily from the latter's aversion to democracy and egalitarianism. Importantly, it points out that "Spencer found little in Nietzsche about the organization of the state."

Spencer's own writings are few, and the only reference we found to Nietzsche was in a speech[16] in which he mentions Nietzsche, along with Copernicus and Martin Luther, as an example of someone who "overturn[s] whole schools of thought and institutions and society's most basic assumptions."

Well, fair enough. Nietzsche was indeed a disruptor and admired disruptors. We are disruptors, and those of you who are reading this book are or intend to be disruptors. This does not address the question of what one is disrupting or what one is offering as a replacement. The author of the Spencer article makes the connection to anti-egalitarianism, but he offers no evidence that Spencer made that same connection. In all, the purported link between Nietzsche and Spencer seems to be much ado about nothing: a relatively minor point in the *Atlantic* article and an example of clickbait philosophy in the articles that reference it.

15 Josh Harkinson, "Meet the White Nationalist Trying to Ride the Trump Train to Lasting Power," *Mother Jones*, October 27, 2016.

16 Richard Spencer, "Facing the Future as a Minority" (American Renaissance conference, April 2013). Video available on YouTube, and a transcript can be found at https://www.theoccidentalobserver.net/2013/05/14/facing-the-future-as-a-minority/

Now, *The Genealogy of Morals* does make reference to the "magnificent blonde beast," the "Aryan race," and in exactly one place, the "master race." This seems menacing until one actually reads the book and realizes it is a lesson in history and etymology, particularly around the words "good," "bad," and "evil." One of Nietzsche's key philosophical contributions is his notion of "master morality" along with the reactive slave morality that spread through Europe in the first few centuries AD. In these worrisome phrases, Nietzsche is referring to the Teutons and Goths, and describing their effect on the rest of the population:

> *The profound, icy mistrust which the German provokes, as soon as he arrives at power,—even at the present time,—is always still an aftermath of that inextinguishable horror with which for whole centuries Europe has regarded the wrath of the blonde Teuton beast (although between the old Germans and ourselves there exists scarcely a psychological, let alone a physical, relationship).[17]*

He does express a kind of admiration for the Teutons, but that does not seem to be his point. Rather, it is to decry the response of everyone else, the rise of slave morality, and what is now known as *ressentiment*. This is all quite complicated, and once you come to understand it, you may find his actual view disagreeable. But in our reading, aided by plenty of secondary sources, Nietzsche's views provide no support to white nationalism.

In an accessible article in *Vox*,[18] Sean Illing (whose doctoral dissertation[19] involved a deep reading of Nietzsche) outlines a view similar

---

17 *The Geneaology of Morals*, Essay 1, section 11.
18 Sean Illing, "The alt-right is drunk on bad readings of Nietzsche. The Nazis were too," *Vox*, August 2017.
19 Sean Illing, "Between nihilism and transcendence: Albert Camus' dialogue with Nietzsche and Dostoevsky" (doctoral dissertation, Louisiana State...

to what we have presented here. He also makes some claims specifically about Spencer and others associated with the alt-right misreading Nietzsche. While this does not prove our view, it supports our skepticism of the association with white nationalism.

MISOGYNY

One may easily find statements about women in Nietzsche's works that are patently offensive by today's standards. His stated views about the appropriate roles for women and his stereotyping of their behavior are manifestly chauvinistic and sexist. For example:

When a woman has scholarly inclinations there is generally something wrong with her sexual nature.[20]

...nothing is more foreign, more repugnant, or more hostile to woman than truth—her great art is falsehood, her chief concern is appearance and beauty.[21]

Woman gives herself, man takes her.[22]

Without debating whether 19th-century male chauvinism constitutes misogyny (from its literal Greek roots, the term refers to an actual hatred of women), one can surely agree that Nietzsche did not manage to transcend the prevailing attitudes of his day, in contrast with

---

...University, 2014). Available at LSU Digital Commons.
20 *Beyond Good and Evil*, section 144.
21 *Beyond Good and Evil*, section 232.
22 *The Joyful Wisdom*, section 363.

his contemporary and foil John Stuart Mill.[23] He nevertheless explicitly calls out the self-hatred of misogynists: "'Woman is our enemy'— The man who speaks to men in this way exhibits an unbridled lust which not only hates itself but also its means."[24]

Occasionally he uses phrasing that seems to more clearly cross the line. The most egregious example is in a chapter from *Thus Spoke Zarathustra*. The chapter includes not only sexist lines such as "everything in woman has one solution—it is called pregnancy" and "Man shall be trained for war, and woman for the recreation of the warrior," but also the widely quoted and worrisome "You go to women? Do not forget the whip!"[25]

In a paper by Professor Higgins[26] and in at least one guidebook on *Thus Spoke Zarathustra*,[27] one learns why interpreting this line as expressing male domination and abuse is fraught and probably incorrect. Remember first that Nietzsche intended *Thus Spoke Zarathustra* to synthesize philosophy with art, a work of fiction heavy in allegory and allusion. The section at issue has a sarcastic and dark comedic tone, and he presents Zarathustra there as a sneaky and uncertain character in conversation with an old woman of ambiguous identity. This less-than-authoritative Zarathustra utters the chauvinistic lines, while the old woman reveals the "whip" comment as a "little truth."

With this context, note that one of the few surviving photographs of Nietzsche is a posed scene with him and friend Paul Rée being "whipped"

---

23 See, for example, Mill's 1869 essay *The Subjection of Women*.
24 *Dawn of Day*, section 346.
25 *Thus Spoke Zarathustra*, Part I, section 18, "Old and Young Women."
26 Kathleen Higgins, "The Whip Recalled," *Journal of Nietzsche Studies* 12, Nietzsche and Women (Autumn 1996): 1–18.
27 Douglas Burnham and Martin Jesinghausen, *Nietzsche's Thus Spoke Zarathustra* (Bloomington, IN: Indiana University Press, 2010).

by Nietzsche's unrequited love interest, famed intellectual Lou Andreas-Salomé. Consequently, one could reasonably interpret the line as a tongue-in-cheek stereotype: when a man is involved with a woman, the woman is in charge. Higgins goes on to illustrate potential intertextual references in this section with Plato's *Symposium* and *Phaedrus*, Schopenhauer's *On Noise*, Apuleius's *The Golden Ass*, and a number of other passages within *Thus Spoke Zarathustra*, all of which make the meaning of the section and the reference to the whip multifaceted and ambiguous.

Casting doubt on misogyny while admitting chauvinism is hardly a ringing endorsement. Can we say anything positive about Nietzsche's view of women or of his philosophy in relation to women?

Nietzsche's notion of perspectivism has become an implicit staple of modern feminism. Perspectivism is the idea that there is no "view from nowhere" that is an objectively correct interpretation of events in the world, a text, or anything else. Many strains of feminism build on this to establish that a woman's differing perspective is not merely an alternative to consider but rather an equally valid view of the world. This has been most dramatically manifested in the application of a "reasonable woman standard" in sexual harassment cases.[28]

---

28 *Ellison v. Brady*, 924 F.2d 872 (9th Cir. 1991).

Perspectivism in Nietzsche is a general concept, and one might therefore see its value to feminism as incidental to his philosophy. But in his discussions of women, Nietzsche emphasizes the conflict in viewpoints with men and the difficulty men have in understanding their view. "Everything in woman is a riddle," he says in that same troubling section of *Thus Spoke Zarathustra*. Imagining that this application of perspectivism escaped his notice is implausible. Thus, despite his own sexism, he would have grasped that women have a different and valid view, even though he does not understand it.

Further, in his various works, Nietzsche uses "woman" as a metaphor for life,[29] wisdom,[30] happiness,[31] and truth.[32] He sees marriage as requiring mutual reverence.[33] In many places, he uses motherhood and child-bearing as a metaphor for the most important elements of his philosophy, such as creativity and the overhuman. Admittedly, all these are in the context of his chauvinistic stereotypes; still, it suggests that he saw women as an important and valuable part of life's equation.

Not surprisingly, there are extensive debates about these topics in both philosophical and feminist academic literature.[34] There is likely no definitive explanation of Nietzsche's true views on women. One might even suspect that Nietzsche himself was torn and inconsistent.[35] It is probably safe to say that he maintained an unenlightened thread

29 *The Joyful Wisdom*, section 339.
30 *Thus Spoke Zarathustra*, Part I, section 7, "Reading and Writing."
31 *Thus Spoke Zarathustra*, Part III, section 47, "Involuntary Bliss."
32 *Beyond Good and Evil*, Preface.
33 *Thus Spoke Zarathustra*, Part I, section 20, "Child and Marriage."
34 For example, Peter Burgard, ed., *Nietzsche and the Feminine* (Charlottesville, VA: University of Virginia Press, 1994).
35 Peter Burgard, "Introduction: Figures of Excess," in *Nietzsche and the Feminine*.

of chauvinism and sexism,[36] typical of men of his era, but also held the feminine to be a crucial part of life's balance. A stronger claim of misogyny is suspect.

OTHER CONCERNS

Nietzsche's notion of the Übermensch (variously translated as superman, overhuman, and other variants) has inspired numerous interpretations. This is not surprising, as his use of the term was almost entirely within *Thus Spoke Zarathustra*, which is a complex fictional and allegorical work of literature. Some of these interpretations, such as eugenics or racial superiority, are concerning. The most common interpretations, though, see it as a kind of aspirational goal for individual humans or possibly for mankind as a whole. In these readings, it is a goal of self-improvement, specifically along the lines of creating new moral and aesthetic values in the face of the world's growing nihilism. Importantly, in the story, there are no actual overhumans to be found, and the character Zarathustra fails repeatedly to achieve this status.

The overman is the antithesis of the "Last Man," who is a kind of slobbering couch potato not unlike characters in the movie *Idiocracy*. Nietzsche speaks frequently and derisively in his non-fiction about the "herd," members of which adhere to the notion of slave morality, discussed earlier. It is difficult to resist reading Nietzsche as an elitist. This elitism emphasizes moral and creative behavior and sometimes intellect, not bloodlines. In other words, on this reading, he was a meritocratic elitist.

What seems to bother people most about this is the fact that Nietzsche is unapologetic about it. In his time, just as now, egalitarian

---

36 Higgins, "The Whip Recalled," 2.

values were a powerful social influence. One is not supposed to see some people as better than others and should especially not see oneself as better. This is a central element of slave morality. But you cannot run a business by hiring people at random. Some of them are better than others, at least in terms of skills, cultural fit, and other factors. We have made use of Nietzsche's anti-egalitarianism in this book as a spur for you to question what all this means for you and your business.

Nietzsche saw democracy as containing the seeds of its own undoing: "modern democracy is the historical form of the decay of the State."[37] But he also derided aristocratic institutions, anarchy, and the German state of his day. He was not a fan of the nation-state at all: "the state tells lies in all the tongues of good and evil; and whatever it says it lies—and whatever it has it has stolen. Everything about it is false; it bites with stolen teeth, and bites easily."[38] His statements on forms of government are infrequent, and we have never seen an argument that he had any sort of positive theory on government. When it comes to politics, Nietzsche was more of a whiner than an advocate.

Between the absence of such a positive theory and his anti-egalitarianism, reading Nietzsche as a Marxist would be quite a stretch. How is it, then, that Nietzsche has been so popular among critical theorists, deconstructionists, postmodernists, and the like, most of whom are least inclined toward, if not all-in on, Marxism? There is probably no simple answer to this, and the literature of critical theory debates the question. Nevertheless, Nietzsche's perspectivism seems to be an important contributor. It gives fuel to many of the ideas of critical theory, more abstractly than the details of politics, and this seems to be one source of interest.

---

37 *Human, All-Too-Human*, section 472.
38 *Thus Spoke Zarathustra*, Part I, "On the New Idol."

The dark side of perspectivism is that one can easily interpret it as relativism, both moral and epistemic. Nietzsche frequently wrote about all our concepts being "illusions" that serve our survival needs but do not reflect underlying truth. Some have used these ideas to justify a "post-truth" viewpoint (on both the political left and right, as well as in other contexts), which is clearly of great concern today. But this is a genuine and lasting philosophical issue—Nietzsche is neither alone nor the first in these ideas. Plato's famous allegory of the cave and Kant's subjective turn are among the predecessors. Nietzsche is particularly influential in this case, in part because his writing is so colorful and compelling.

CONCLUSION

We have made the case here that reliance on Nietzsche to justify any point of view is suspect, and in particular we have focused on some of the more offensive ideas people have tried to attribute to him. We do not put credence into any strong claims about Nietzsche's positions, and we try not to make any ourselves.

Despite the difficulties in ascribing clear positions to Nietzsche, for the record, we can speak definitively and clearly about our own views. Neither the authors nor (to our knowledge) any of the contributors to this book endorse or find remotely acceptable the reprehensible racist, sexist, and xenophobic views of the alt-right, white nationalists, neo-Nazis, or related groups.

APPENDIX 3

SOURCES

Here we provide the source for the Nietzsche quote from each chapter. We have cited by section or number as applicable to each book. We do this instead of using page numbers so that readers who delve deeper are not tied to particular translations or editions. The majority of the quotes in our text either comprise the entirety of the original section or aphorism, or just omit its brief title. A few, especially those from *Thus Spoke Zarathustra*, are taken from longer passages.

Nietzsche wrote exclusively in German, so we have also included the English translator and date for each work. The full public domain works are available on *Gutenberg.org* or, in some cases, as free eBooks on Google Books or Amazon. There are also more modern translations available. Stanford University Press is working its way through a 21st-century translation of his complete works.

BOOKS AND TRANSLATIONS

Thoughts out of Season (sometimes translated as *Untimely Meditations*) was published in 1876. We have used the 1910 translation by Anthony Ludovici.

Human, All-Too-Human: A Book for Free Spirits was first published in 1878. Nietzsche subsequently added *Miscellaneous Maxims and Opinions* in 1879 and *The Wanderer and His Shadow* in 1880. Because each of these three major sections has its own numbering scheme for the sections/aphorisms, we have indicated the major section. For the original book, except as noted, we have used the 1909 translation by Helen Zimmern. For the other two sections, we used the 1913 translation by Paul V. Cohn.

The Dawn of Day (sometimes translated as *Daybreak*) was published in 1881. We have used the 1911 translation by John McFarland Kennedy.

The Joyful Wisdom (sometimes translated as *The Gay Science*) was published in 1882. We have used the 1910 translation by Thomas Common.

Thus Spake Zarathustra: A Book for All and None (usually just called *Thus Spoke Zarathustra*, the convention we have adopted here) was originally published in parts, with the first three parts published together in 1882. The book was not published with the fourth part until 1892. We have used the 1909 translation by Thomas Common. While this translation has been criticized for errors in conveying Nietzsche's philosophical intent, it nevertheless offers an archaic, biblical style that was part of his literary intent. In a few cases, we have replaced some of the archaic terms with modern words.

Beyond Good and Evil was published in 1886. Except as noted, we have used the 1906 translation by Helen Zimmern.

The Genealogy of Morals: A Polemic was published in 1887. Except as noted, we have used the 1913 translation by Horace B. Samuel.

In two cases, we assembled a custom translation based on multiple sources. For *Delight in Yourself*, we combined the Zimmern translation with the 1986 translation by Marion Faber, along with our own language. For *Strong Beliefs*, we synthesized the Samuel translation with a version of the quote found in a 1988 translation of Lou Andreas-Salome's *Nietzsche*, by Elise and Theo Mandel.

STRATEGY

Domination: *Human, All-Too-Human—The Wanderer and His Shadow #344*
Finding Your Way: *Thus Spoke Zarathustra Part III, Chapter LV, The Spirit of Gravity*
Doing the Obvious: *Human, All-Too-Human—The Wanderer and His Shadow #347*
Overcoming Obstacles: *The Dawn of Day #444*
Patience in Disruption: *The Dawn of Day #534*
Hitting Bottom: *Thus Spoke Zarathustra Part III, Chapter XLV, The Wanderer*
Silent Killers: *Thus Spoke Zarathustra Part II, Chapter XL, Great Events*
Seeing the Future: *Human, All-Too-Human—The Wanderer and His Shadow #330*
Information: *The Joyful Wisdom #41*
Milestones: *Human, All-Too-Human—The Wanderer and His Shadow #204*
Planning: *Human, All-Too-Human—Miscellaneous Maxims and Opinions #85*

CULTURE

Trust: *Beyond Good and Evil #183*
Gratitude: *The Joyful Wisdom #100*
Persistence: *Beyond Good and Evil #72*
Surpassing: *Thus Spoke Zarathustra Part II, Chapter XXXIV, Self-Surpassing*
Style: *Thoughts out of Season, David Strauss, The Confessor and the Writer, Section 1*
Consequences: *Beyond Good and Evil #179*
Monsters: *Beyond Good and Evil #146*
Groupthink: *Beyond Good and Evil #156*
Independence of Mind: *The Joyful Wisdom #32*
Maturity: *Human, All-Too-Human—Miscellaneous Maxims and Opinions #283*
Integrators: *Human, All-Too-Human—The Wanderer and His Shadow #76*

FREE SPIRITS

Deviance: *Human, All-Too-Human #224*
Obsession: *The Joyful Wisdom #55*
Work as Reward: *The Joyful Wisdom #42*

Delight in Yourself: *Human, All-Too-Human #501*
Maturity as Play: *Beyond Good and Evil #94*
Genius: *Human, All-Too-Human—Miscellaneous Maxims and Opinions #378*
Wisdom from Experience: *Human, All-Too-Human—The Wanderer and His Shadow #298*
Serial Entrepreneurship: *The Joyful Wisdom #163*
Shadow of Success: *Beyond Good and Evil #269*
Reflecting Your Light: *Human, All-Too-Human—Miscellaneous Maxims and Opinions #61*

LEADERSHIP

Taking Responsibility: *Beyond Good and Evil #68*
Doing Is Not Leading: *Human, All-Too-Human #521*
Faith: *Human, All-Too-Human—The Wanderer and His Shadow #234*
Attracting Followers: *Human, All-Too-Human—The Wanderer and His Shadow #254*
Resolute Decisions: *Beyond Good and Evil #107*
Right Messages: *Beyond Good and Evil #99*
Leading Gently: *The Joyful Wisdom #216*
Gratitude and Integrity: *Beyond Good and Evil #74*
Two Types of Leaders: *The Dawn of Day #554*
Introverts: *Thus Spoke Zarathustra Part II, XLIV, The Stillest Hour*

TACTICS

Once More with Feeling: *Beyond Good and Evil #128*
Play to the Audience: *Human, All-Too-Human #177*
Show the Value: *Human, All-Too-Human #533*
Strong Beliefs: *The Genealogy of Morals Essay 3, #24*
Transparency: *Thus Spoke Zarathustra Part III, Chapter L, On the Olive-Mount*
Red Hot: *Beyond Good and Evil #91*
Imitators: *The Joyful Wisdom #255*
Stepping Back: *Human, All-Too-Human—The Wanderer and His Shadow #307*
Sustaining Intensity: *Human, All-Too-Human—Miscellaneous Maxims and Opinions #266*
Cleaning Up: *Human, All-Too-Human—The Wanderer and His Shadow #335*

ACKNOWLEDGMENTS

Maureen Amundson and Amy Batchelor are our life and intellectual partners. In the course of writing this book (and everything else we do), they supported us and they gave us advice and ideas. We are grateful to have them in our lives.

The book would be much inferior without the narratives contributed by many entrepreneurs. Each of them was willing to consider what would be their most helpful story and, in most cases, to be vulnerable in sharing it. They spent time writing and working through several iterations of the text. We thank each of you for your contribution: Ingrid Alongi, Daniel Benhammou, Matt Blumberg, Sal Carcia, Ben Casnocha, Ralph Clark, David Cohen, Mat Ellis, Tim Enwall, Nicole Glaros, Will Herman, Mike Kail, Luke Kanies, Walter Knapp, Gary LaFever, Tracy Lawrence, Jenny Lawton, Seth Levine, Bart Lorang, David Mandell, Jason Mendelson, Tim Miller, Matt Munson, Ted Myerson, Bre Pettis, Laura Rich, Jacqueline Ros, Jud Valeski, and one more who, because of the sensitivity of his story, had to remain anonymous.

Reid Hoffman took the time to understand exactly what we were trying to accomplish with this book, and wrote a foreword that both introduces and gracefully adds to what we have done. We are very grateful for his insights.

Numerous people read and commented on early drafts of the book. These include Will Herman, Kristin Lindquist, Dina Supino, Jamey Sperans, Rajat Bhargava, Ben Casnocha, Greg Gottesman, Peter Birkeland, Rachel Meier, and Maureen Amundson. Their feedback helped us identify some weaknesses early on that made this a much better book.

CPSIA information can be obtained
at www.ICGtesting.com
Printed in the USA
LVHW091330051121
702222LV00021B/183/J

9 781544 521411